The Schemes
of Satan

PTLB
PRINCIPLES
TO LIVE BY
LIFE IS RELATIONSHIPS

Gil Stieglitz

The Schemes of Satan

Building Strong Christians for the Battle

© 2015 Gil Stieglitz

Published by Principles to Live By, Roseville, CA 95661

www.ptlb.com

Cover by John Chase

Copyedited by Jennifer Edwards and Sandy Johnson

Scripture verses are from the New American Standard Bible unless otherwise indicated.

New American Standard Bible: 1995 update.

1995 La Habra, CA: The Lockman Foundation.

ISBN 978-0-9909641-4-8

Christian Living

Printed in the United States of America

Dedication

The book is dedicated to one of my mentors,
a true warrior for Christ:

Neil Anderson

and

Freedom in Christ Ministries

For 30+ years Neil has fought the good fight by turning
people toward the truths of Christ, freeing them from the
bondage of Satan.

Thank you!

Contents

Introduction

What are the Schemes of Satan?

Satan is alive and well and living on planet earth. Every day he strategizes how to destroy people's lives through the tests and temptations he runs. One of them is that people must choose to sin and want the Devil's malevolent influence in their lives. The more selfishness people choose, the more selfishness they can be tempted with. So the Devil makes the wrong choices seem right. He glamorizes absolutely toxic opportunities.

We actually face three enemies that want to block us from enjoying the life God has planned for us: The World (1 John 2:15-18); The Flesh (Gal. 5:19-21); The Devil (Eph. 6:10-18). Each of these enemies can get in the way of embracing the great life and good works that God has planned for us (Eph. 2:10). In this book we will be focusing on just the last of these enemies—the Devil, paying particular attention to what his strategies are to rob us of God's abundant life. The Devil wants to amplify our desires, our emotions, our selfishness, and our interest in power and wisdom until he can control us through those amplified elements. You will notice in the various schemes that Satan runs an amplification theme. He wants us to embrace a way of living that is not normal. He wants to lure us away from the life we could have through an over emphasis on one or two issues, ideas, emotions or desires.

In 2 Corinthians 2, the Apostle Paul says, "We are not ignorant of the Devil's strategies." Sadly, in our present world this is not the case. A good deal of time must be spent educating people on how the Devil seeks to trip them up. I am always troubled when people fall for fake blessings and foolish choices. The strategies of the Devil consistently work on the unaware. I see it happen all the time. An individual finds comfort at the bottom of a bottle rather than in a relationship that could really help. A man thinks he has found meaning and joy in pornography rather than with a real woman and true soul intimacy. A woman trades the safety of her present life for the excitement of a relationship with a dangerous man. A man chases after a get-rich-quick scheme, rather than learn the discipline and practices that will provide more than adequate resources without the anxiety. A person embraces the possibility that everything could go wrong and lives in fear, causing them to make little positive impact. This is what the Devil specializes in—robbing us of the life we could have by distracting us with a fake pleasure or an empty accomplishment. We are like people at the carnival paying five dollars to throw darts at balloons to win toys only worth a dollar.

I just read a report from the notorious criminal and mob boss, Whitey Bulger, where he acknowledged that he wasted his life. "Crime does not pay," he said. He recognized that he had the chance for a much better life even as his brother went on to become a positive political figure in Massachusetts. He, however, chose impulsively, wickedly, and selfishly time after time until he wasted his life. Whitey was correct that he had wasted his life—his choices were bad. There were societal factors, personal factors, and spiritual factors influencing him; but he made the choices. His best possible future had been robbed from him (by his own choices), and at the end of his life, he knew he blew it.

Understanding Spiritual Warfare

If one is going to understand what is happening to them, it is very important to realize what the Devil is doing. He doesn't want a person to enjoy a loving, positive life where they fulfill God's mission for their life. The Devil really does want people to fail, to waste their life, and to miss God's best.

> *Be of sober spirit, be on the alert. Your adversary, the Devil, prowls around like a roaring lion, seeking someone to devour. (1 Pet. 5:8)*

It is clear from the Scriptures that the best possible future is a relationally rich life full of love (Matt. 22:37-39) and personally significant good works (Eph. 2:10). The commandments that are elevated by Christ are to love God, to love others, and to love oneself (righteously). If these are the highest commands, then this is where we are to aim. Success has been achieved when our lives are full of loving relationships. Contrarily, if you are wealthy or powerful but without people who love you and whom you love, then your life has been a failure. I remember hearing of a rich doctor who was a horrible boss and a taskmaster to his wife and children. Eventually, everyone wanted to get away from him and they did. When he sold his business to retire, no one had to spend time with him anymore, so no one ever came to see him. His family shunned him and he was alone. He was very wealthy, but he died alone. His body was not discovered for a week since nobody checked on him regularly. The Devil had helped this man make choices that robbed him of the very success that he was working so hard to obtain. His piles of money did him no good because he was such a selfish and disagreeable person.

The Schemes of Satan

The Bible reveals the basic schemes of Satan which I have listed below. These are revealed in the Scriptures through the various titles given to Satan, the angelic being Lucifer, who corrupted himself and became what we know of as the Devil and Satan. There are over twenty-two different titles God gives to Satan that I have grouped into eight basic types. In this way it is easier to perceive the scheme he is running. You can more easily keep track of eight schemes than all twenty two. Each scheme is designed to get us off track and to have us miss God's best in some way. Satan wants us to waste our life on something other than what God had planned for us (Eph. 2:10). He does not really care which schemes you fall for, just that you do not fulfill God's purpose for your life or live out Christ's abundant life for you (John 10:10).

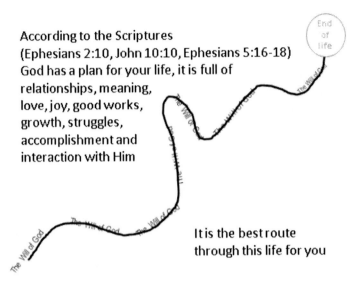

According to the Scriptures
(Ephesians 2:10, John 10:10, Ephesians 5:16-18)
God has a plan for your life, it is full of
relationships, meaning,
love, joy, good works,
growth, struggles,
accomplishment and
interaction with Him

End of life

It is the best route
through this life for you

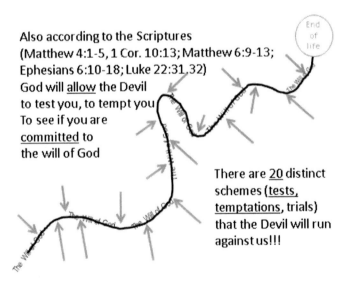

Also according to the Scriptures
(Matthew 4:1-5, 1 Cor. 10:13; Matthew 6:9-13;
Ephesians 6:10-18; Luke 22:31,32)
God will allow the Devil
to test you, to tempt you
To see if you are
committed to
the will of God

End of life

There are 20 distinct
schemes (tests,
temptations, trials)
that the Devil will run
against us!!!

Let's take a look at these eight schemes:

1. The Tempter Scheme (Amplified Desire)

In this scheme, the Devil and his demons try and amplify a normal desire to excessive proportions. Normal desires consist of things like the need to be noticed by others, comfort and ability to fit in with your peers, a say in your life, sexual fulfillment in marriage, rest and recreation, food and drink, and money to live life. But these can be amplified so that we feel the need for fame, the latest gadgets, power to make others do what we want, sexual release outside of marriage, engaging in little or no work, overindulgence in food, drink, freedom from all pain, and money to pursue all our desires.

2. The Devil Scheme (Amplified Lies, Accusation)

In this scheme, the Devil and his demons weave an elaborate deception in order to accuse someone and have you think it's true. The Devil will lie and create doubt about people, the truth, or good organizations and then bring slander, rumor, gossip, and false accusations against them. One of the Devil's favorite targets of this scheme is *you*. He brings a withering critique of your every move to discourage you and keep you from doing God's good work.

3. The Satan Scheme: (Amplified Opposition, Resistance)

In this scheme, Satan and his demons oppose your progress toward good things, good people, and good works. He will oppose you internally and externally through other people and organizations. This is designed to stop you from doing something good and fulfilling your destiny. There are normal amounts of resistance and opposition, but the Satan Scheme is when this is stepped up to another level.

4. The Roaring Lion Scheme (Amplified Fear)

In this scheme, the Devil and his demons try to paralyze you with fear and/or terror. Everyone is afraid of something, and the Devil will try and control your choices and actions through fear. If he can get you to back off of good works, good relationships, and good deeds because of possible fears that could come if you move in that direction, then he has accomplished what he is after. Fear is a normal emotion but the Devil will try and dial your fears up to a level that paralyses you or moves you away from God's best.

5. The Angel of Light Scheme (Amplified Power and Wisdom through illicit spiritual means)

Here, the Devil and his demons present spiritual power and wisdom so that a person is enamored with it and wants to use it for their own ends. In this scheme, people see an angel giving them information that heads them in a new direction away from what God wants for them. This scheme feels like you are being let behind the curtain, so you follow and believe; but really it is a path to destruction.

6. The Dragon Scheme (Amplified Anger)

This scheme amplifies your need for control through anger, violence, and oppression until you become a dragon to others. The Devil and his demons make you feel like you are right to be this angry. They make you feel like you are justified to use violence to accomplish your goals. And they can even make you feel right to murder another person.

7. The Underworld Scheme: (Amplified Sin)

In this scheme, the Devil and his demons expose a person to an underworld life to the point that they become comfortable with it. This includes underworld behaviors, powers, and people. He lets people see underworld power, both natural and supernatural. There are people who have no morals and will do anything for what they want; these are underworld people. He wants to make it seem like this is your world -- a "normal" neighborhood in which you know the rules -- but it is really a manure pile. After a while you begin to believe that this is the only world you can survive in.

8. The God of This World Scheme (Amplified Importance)

Everyone wants to feel important but using this scheme the Devil and his demons convince you, that your need for importance is more significant than others, so you can be excused for doing oppressive, unethical, and evil things to gain or keep control. You really deserve to be the god of this little world you have created. The whispers of this scheme build you up and make you believe that you deserve the control, the obedience, and the accolades of those in your world even if you have to get them through coercion, deception, oppression, affliction, and destruction. He wants you to be satisfied with a puffed up level of importance in a particular world rather than being blessed at a higher level through humility, empathy, love, and learning.

We will explore these eight schemes in much more detail so that we can effectively resist what Satan is doing to destroy our lives. Just reading the above descriptions may have already clued you in to a scheme that the Devil has been running against you. Realize that God does want to bless you with the plan He laid out from before the foundation of the world. The Devil wants to push you off of God's plan and diminish your life. My hope is that this book will help you to choose wisely and live a life that honors God.

Spiritual Exercise

Look over the list of schemes and think back through your life. Can you see whether the Devil used any of these schemes on you in the past? Can you see if the Devil has used these strategies to get you off the right path and on to a destructive side path? List which ones you identify below.

1.

2.

3.

4.

5.

Look over the list of schemes and see if any of these issues, emotions, desires, or kinds of people show up in your life right now. Can you see the Devil using any of these schemes on you in the present? If the answer is "yes," then the Devil is running that scheme against you right now.

Become aware of it so that you can resist him and make him flee. Until you demonstrate that you will not fall for a particular scheme, the Devil will keep using it. List them below.

1.

2.

3.

4.

5.

The Devil really does want you to use your own choices against you. There are God's choices that bring life, wholeness, and benefit to others and then there are sinful, selfish choices that can ruin your life. Right now the Devil is scheming and plotting about how to destroy your life through your own bad choices. Our job is to take up the Armor of God provided by Jesus Christ's life, death, resurrection, and present work in heaven. The Armor of God is truth, righteousness, peace, faith, salvation, Word of God, prayer, and alertness. We will learn more about how to do this in the pages that follow.

Claim the life God has planned for you. Do not allow the Devil to keep you from God's best for your life.

Scheme #1

The Tempter Scheme

(Amplified Desire)

Jerry was a delightful person and full of life and real love for the hurting and oppressed. He was always there to help out and was usually the life of any party he found himself in. He should have seen it coming, but he didn't. His desire to help others allowed him to care so much for people that the Devil took advantage of his desire to help. One day he went to help a young couple that was walking through the stages of grief over the impending death of the husband. The husband had terminal cancer and the end was nearing. He helped them develop a plan for saying goodbye and even the details of the funeral. He comforted everyone, including the soon-to-be young widow. Through that process a subtle shift began to take place from care and righteous comfort to romantic and even sexual interest in the young lady. She was vulnerable and needed (even wanted) every form of comfort, so it was not surprising that she developed feelings for this delightful man who was helping her and her husband through these awful goodbyes. Jerry allowed the Devil to amplify the normal desires to give comfort until it was a raging sexual fire in his soul for this woman who needed him so much. He followed the Tempter's siren song and left his wife and children to give more comfort to this woman. He destroyed his life because the Devil successfully ran the scheme of Excessive Desire from an unexpected angle.

The first scheme of Satan we want to explore is *The Excessive Desire Scheme.* This is one of first ways that everyone experiences the Devil. His trick is in luring us to want something too much. A desire that takes you out of the will of God is excessive even if it seems delightful and exciting. The Devil is called the Tempter because he seeks to lure people away from righteous activities that will build a great and loving life toward selfish pursuits and destructive activities that will destroy potential (Matt. 4:3). There are all kinds of things that tempt us to leave the path of righteousness: fame, power, money, sex, love, vengeance, etc. The Devil as Tempter is testing your commitment to righteousness. Will you say no to something you clearly want? In order for the Devil to tempt you to excess he has to be pulling on something that you actually do want. No one is tempted by what they don't want. I don't know anyone who is lured by the opportunity to have unlimited brussel sprouts!

Desire is not wrong; but excessive desire is often a pathway to harm, missed opportunity, and lost time. I had a friend who "discovered" marijuana in high school and completely embraced the party scene. He kept turning down opportunities to go to college and get better jobs because he was "all good." In the blink of an eye ten years had passed. His friends had graduated from college and begun their families and careers while he was still attending parties with the local high school students chasing the next high. It was such a waste. His life was completely about an excessive desire for a particular feeling. Let me say again that desire is not wrong. In fact, God has given us desires and emotions so that life can be wonderful. We figure out what life is supposed to look like through normal levels of desire. One person desires to spend time with animals and becomes a veterinarian. One person desires to have a family so they get married and start a family earlier than others. One person really enjoys music so they go into the music business. Our desires are not wrong as long as they stay within righteous boundaries. The Devil, though, wants us to take this righteous normal desire and expand it until it is takes us beyond the boundaries of God or until it consumes everything in our life.

He does this by flooding your soul with thoughts, feelings, or willfulness that you "must have" what you just enjoyed (or think you would enjoy). It can be overwhelming when every part of your soul and body is alive with the desire for popularity, revenge, sex, control, sleep, to be left alone, love, money, power, or independence. If we give into this amplification of normal desires, we can be led to lots of places that we would not normally go. This is the heart of the Devil's scheme. He wants you pursuing something that you really don't need as much as he makes you believe you do.

The word in the Scriptures for excessive desire is *epithumia,* which we translate into *lust.* In our culture we tend to see lust as a sexual thing, but sex is not the only excessive desire. In fact, when the Devil was sent to tempt Jesus in Matthew 4, he never suggested sexual temptation (I think he assumed that Jesus would never fall for that type of temptation). The Devil tempted Jesus with fame, power, food, and rebellion. He wanted to see if Jesus could be lured away from the righteous pathway that God the Father had set him on through an excessive desire for popularity, for power, for food, and for the expression of his deity without waiting for the Father and the Spirit. These temptations were tests to see if Jesus would give in to excessive desire. Jesus the Christ passed each test and turned away from the temptations. We also must turn away from the excessive desires that Satan spins for us.

The Devil as Tempter means that he lures us with something we want in order to move us off the righteous path. A person is living their life doing righteous, loving things and then the Devil comes and tells us that we can have more of something we really enjoy. We may realize that we shouldn't have too much of that thing or have it in that way, but it is very desirable and we feel the pull of temptation. Notice the use of the words "tempted, and tempter" in Matthew 4:1-3.

> *Then Jesus was led up by the Spirit into the wilderness to be **tempted** by the Devil. And after he had fasted forty days and forty nights, He then became hungry. And the **tempter** came and said to Him, "If You are the Son of God, command that these stones become bread."*

This word *tempt* is the Greek word *peiradzo*, which means test, tempt, or trial. When the Devil tempts us, it is both a test and a trial. God wants us to pass the test, while the Devil wants us to fail. The Devil is given the titles of Tempter, Tester, and Bringer of Trials in this passage. The Devil is trying to lure Jesus away from complete dependence upon God the Father and God the Holy Spirit. If he can get Jesus to leave the righteous path that God the Father set him on to become the Savior of the world, then the Devil wins. Jesus only had to choose one wrong thing to leave the path of righteousness. He only had to give into the lure of excessive desire. The Devil did not use money or sex to tempt Jesus; instead he used hunger, fame, and power. The Devil failed miserably in trying to tempt Christ, but he often succeeds with us. He wants us to move beyond the normal desires of righteous living and go after excessive desires.

Internal and External Versions

The Devil delivers his schemes either internally or externally. An internal scheme means using thoughts, feelings, willfulness, and choices to turn you toward unrighteous behavior. In this area of excessive desire, he makes you believe that you need something you don't really need and gets you to pursue it. An internal scheme may be that he will drop an excessive desire through an idea, an emotion, or an attitude into our soul to see if we will embrace it as our own. If we choose to own these excessive desires that come from him, then he has planted a hook inside us and can turn us this way and that way by exciting these thoughts, feelings, willfulness, and choices.

If the Devil brings his schemes externally, then an excessive desire comes through the thoughts, feelings, willfulness, and choices of friends, music, social media, heroes, games, advertising, books, authorities, movies, institutions, experts, and in rare instances, objects.

Look at 1 Thessalonians 3:5 and feel the Apostle Paul's great concern that the Devil will be able to lure the new Christians away from their faith with excessive desire.

For this reason, when I could endure it no longer, I also sent to find out about your faith, for fear that the tempter might have tempted you, and our labor would be in vain.

Paul is truly concerned that the people in Thessalonica will be turned aside from their purity of belief and actions of love by the temptations of the Devil. All of us have desires that are a part of living. These are not the problem; it is when we are moved toward excessive desires that the problems start.

The ancient church categorized many of these areas where the Devil amplifies normal desire into the seven deadly sins: pride, envy, anger, lust, sloth, gluttony, and greed. They saw these as primary ways that the Devil tempts us to abandon our best possible life. For many people they need to take stock of their desires and make sure that they have not let any of them become excessive. Let's look at the basic list that the ancient church gave us.

Pride

Pride is an excessive desire for respect. When it comes to pride, it is not wrong to want to be liked; but it causes all kinds of problems when you want to be liked too much. The Devil wants to amplify our normal need for respect and get us to pursue an excessive desire for attention, authority, or self-focus. *People who have a normal desire for respect can forget about themselves for a long period of time and focus on others and their needs.* People who are proud are self-focused. They have a predominant desire to talk and think about themselves. They can have a positive self-focus (I am wonderful) or a negative self-focus (woe is me); a cynical self-focus (everyone is against me), or even a health related self-focus (monitoring every discomfort, illness, bump, or bruise). People who are proud can also allow their amplified desire for respect to move toward a need to be noticed. They have an insatiable desire for popularity, attention, and fame. Another way that an excessive need for respect can manifest is through perceiving the interactions with others as full of disrespect. It is possible that occasionally someone would send disrespecting messages; but if you see it everywhere, it is probably a sign that your need for respect has been amplified to an excessive degree.

Now let me balance our discussion of respect and pride with a healthy look at humility and respect. Every person needs respect. If a person receives no respect from the people and society around them, they live in a most desperate form of poverty. To be a good Christian is to give and receive respect. There are times when you have to fight for a reasonable amount of respect as a person, as a man, as a woman, or as a teenager. This is not being proud; it is asking for a normal amount of respect that may have in the past been denied. The basic definition of humility means that you can focus on others and not just yourself.

Envy

Envy is an inordinate desire for status, things, and relationships that others have. It is not wrong to notice that others have a nice life, marriage, job, etc. It becomes wrong when we fixate on what they have to the point where we must have what they have or who they have. When we see others succeeding, it can serve as a role model for our own diligence and goals. But when it becomes an excessive desire, we are not okay unless we have what they have, whether that means with their not having it or us having more or better than what they have. This is envy. In our material world it can clearly drive people to waste their whole life trying to compete with or take what is someone else's blessings. It is so common for people who give themselves to this excessive desire to proclaim "Is this all there is?" once they obtain the object of their affection.

The Devil can get us chasing these stupid goals and ignoring the righteous off-ramps that God has given us for a great life. No, we must have that thing (car, bike, degree, person) that we fixated on when we were kids. No, we must have that job or relationship that got those other people so much popularity. Do not chase someone else's life. Instead, hunger and thirst after righteousness. Chase your own righteous life. God has planned out good works for you to do that are specific to you. Do those. They will result in a great life with great people and great accomplishments.

Anger

Anger is an excessive desire to have our expectations met. It is not wrong to want to have our expectations met as long as we understand that it will not always happen. When we want all our expectations to be met all the time, then it is likely there is an anger problem. Getting irritated and even mad because the world and everyone in it does not immediately jump to help us achieve our expectations indicates a serious problem. The problem is that Satan is leading us around by the nose! If every time you have an expectation you think should be met, you have an unrealistic picture of the world that the Devil can use against you.

Now, let me tell you that many times you may have the right expectation; but it is still unrealistic because of the people involved, your level of communication, the circumstances, the lack of planning, etc. Our desires can become expectations so quickly that we can be manipulated by the Devil. How many people do you know who can be angry or irritated at the drop of a hat? The food was not just right; the driver in the other lane did not signal; the person put you on hold; your spouse was late; your sports team lost a close game; the other political party won; your children acted like children and made a mess; and so on.

Lust

Lust is inordinate desire for sexual expression outside of God's plan. It is not wrong to want sex, but when it doesn't matter who you have it with and there is no loving public commitment, it has become an excessive desire that will damage you and others. How do we know if our desire for sexual expression is excessive? First, ask yourself if it is within God's approved container for sexual expression—marriage? If you want to express your sexual desires outside of a loving lifetime relationship with your spouse, then your desire is excessive. All form of adultery is by definition excessive desire. I am deeply saddened by the number of people who have a sexual desire pop up within their mind to spend time sexually with someone who is not their spouse, and they don't recognize that it's an excessive desire and a test from the Devil! It doesn't matter who or how pleasurable it would be or if they are interested or whatever; if it is outside of the duly sanctioned marriage relationship of one man with one woman, then that desire will be destructive. If you go with it, you will have failed the test. More tests will follow and your corruption will push forward until it has destroyed your life.

If you are not married, then you need to hold on to your sexual expression until you can find an opposite sex partner whom you can share your life with in a marriage. Do not let yourself be led astray by Satan who tells you that there is meaning, purpose, and unending joy in sexual expression as an end in itself. It is just not there. You will be too distracted by new sexual conquests that you'll go down a path of diminishing returns, ultimately causing you to miss God's best for you.

Sloth

Sloth is the inordinate desire for rest, comfort, sleep, and ease. It is not wrong to want to rest and get adequate sleep but when most things are put off until tomorrow and necessary issues are not handled, you have an excessive desire called laziness, and it will destroy your potential. Do you find yourself regularly turning down opportunities because it would be too hard or you want to take it easy? Have you begun to baby yourself to the point where hard work, effort, or discomfort is unacceptable? It is normal to want to rest, sleep, and have comfort but that cannot become the fixation of our lives. We need to work in order to have a sense of accomplishment. Do not let a sudden thought of rest or flood of feelings that "this is too hard" keep you from pushing forward on a path you know is right. Yes, there is overwork and there are people who never take breaks; but if you are worried about that, then that is probably not you. The people who really do work too much rarely ever realize they need a break. They are usually looking to add more things.

Gluttony

Gluttony is an inordinate desire for food, drink, some substance (drugs), or activity. It is not wrong to enjoy food and drink; but when you are always thinking about your next meal or next drink, then you have an excessive desire and this will punish you over time. It usually becomes excessive because it dulls the pain in your soul so you don't have to face some wound or trauma. The Devil is all too willing to offer a drug, alcohol, food, porn, or sex so that you do not ever deal with the trauma, wound, or damage that is sitting unresolved in your soul. Gluttony is a desire to dodge the real issues of life.

Some have sought to fight the desire for food, drink, drugs, or whatever and usually this plan alone fails because there is a soul pain that must be faced and dealt with before the temptation can be removed. When the Devil comes, the Tempter is trying to lure you to eat too much, drink too much, take drugs (legal and illegal); and this seems like a good thing, but you have a bigger issue. What are you trying to run away from? There must be some wound that maybe you have not really wanted to talk about or face. If a wound is not there driving the gluttony, then your desire for the food, drink, or drugs will not be strong enough. These things will not be tempting.

Greed

Greed is an inordinate desire for money. It is not wrong to want money to live your life, but it becomes wrong when you have an excessive love for money to the point where money becomes a primary goal and constant desire (1 Tim. 6:10,11). The Devil comes and helps us believe the promises that if we just had more money, everything would be great. This is not true, but so many of us want to believe it. He comes by with a get-rich-quick scheme or a deal in which you only have to bend the rules a little. He offers you a job that you would hate or are not suited for but it pays a huge amount of money. The Devil offers you the chance to make a lot of money if you pay others less than what they deserve. He gives you the chance to become rich if you will be okay with cheating, lying, or stealing from others. In Proverbs 23,

Solomon clearly says, "Do not weary yourself to gain wealth, cease from your consideration of it. When you set your eyes on it, it is gone. For wealth certainly makes itself wings like an eagle that flies toward the heavens." There is nothing wrong with money; it is the excessive desire for it that corrupts. Listen to what God says through the Apostle Paul about the lust for money, "For the love of money is a root of all sorts of evil, and some by longing for it have wandered away from the faith and pierced themselves with many grief's." (1 Tim. 6:10)

Everyone wants to provide for themselves and their family. Some people are able to earn and provide a lot, but their focus cannot be on the money they will make. It must be on the service they will provide or the good work they are doing. Money is just compensation for loving others well.

This is one way the Devil pulls us off the path to our best future. He amplifies our desire in one or more areas so that we stop making progress with our skills, talents, and righteous relationships. We stop helping others and we stop building a positive relational life. It all becomes about getting more of the thing we lust after: respect, power, fame, control, money, food, sex, vengeance, your way, rest, alcohol, drugs, and so on. When the Devil has you chasing one thing because you are convinced that it is the key to pleasure, peace, joy, and fulfillment, then he has won. You get off the righteous path to chase the one thing and head to a desert place. There is no meaning there, only momentary pleasure. There are usually very little meaningful relationships there, only the thing we have to have. Haven't we all watched people who tried to eat themselves out of a setback or depression only to land in a deeper problem with their weight or addiction? We have all known wonderful people who followed the siren call of alcohol, drugs, money, food, or sex to a lonely place that changed them and damaged their life.

Hear me when I say that it is not wrong to want respect; justice; met expectations; a committed loving sexual relationship; rest and sleep; adequate food, drink, and happiness; and resources to live your life. It is the excessive desire for these needs that destroys the good life. Most people are only tempted by three or four of the seven deadly sins; the others not so much. It is important to realize the areas where we are susceptible to a temptation that could lead to excessive desire. It is these few areas of potential excessive desire that the Devil and his demons focus on to derail our lives.

Let me give you a few examples where I have seen this take place. Having talked with a number of men in prison, it is often an excessive desire that lured them to make a foolish choice that landed them in prison in the first place. They wanted easy money, the pretty underage girl, to express their rage fully, went after what someone else had, and had to prove how tough or powerful they were. I have also talked with too many young ladies who jumped into a sexual relationship with a good-looking man before discovering whether he was a good man. I have heard the tales of woe from dozens of people who chased money through get-rich-quick schemes or illegal enterprises.

I worked with a man who was fixating on more money than he was receiving through his normal job. Of course the Devil arranged for him to have conversations with people who had great sounding get-rich-quick schemes. His dreams of more money were being amplified into a constant drumbeat in his head. He could have more money, and he could have it quickly if he just bent the rules a little or risked money he couldn't afford to lose. The Bible clearly says that if you are going to get rich (although that is not a great goal), one should get rich slowly lest it corrupt you in your pursuit of it.

I have worked with a number of pastors who have a hard time admitting that their desire for a bigger church was an excessive desire. They wanted more people to come hear their sermons, but they clearly did not have (and were not willing to learn) the leadership, communication, or shepherding skills to support that size of congregation. Some applied for new congregations that were larger so that they could have the respect that they craved. Usually they grew their church down to the level of their present abilities rather than growing themselves up to the leadership size to really help this new congregation. The goal of life is not fame, power, or prestige but a relationally loving and full-life present to Jesus Christ for his approval. Yes, we should reach as many people as possible; but God will not answer the Devil's amplification of our desire for respect when it becomes pride and vanity.

I talk with many people who are upset or depressed because God has not answered their prayers for something that comes out of an excessive desire. The Devil may be tempting you to desperately want something that you really should moderate. One young single man I knew desperately wanted to be married and have a committed sexual relationship. He had the opportunity for many normal relationships that could move toward marriage, but instead he fixated upon a few incredibly beautiful women who he could never attract into a relationship. He blamed God for not answering his prayers when it was the Devil who was amplifying his normal desires for a committed, loving relationship to the point where he would only settle for marrying a super attractive woman.

The Devil doesn't have to show up in a red suit with a pitchfork. He only has to amplify your desire for something until there is no way it can deliver what you need it to do in your life.

Resisting the Tempter

The Need for Confession

Many people do not realize that they have already moved from a normal desire to an excessive desire. It may seem like a normal level of desire to you but to others they recognize that it is an excessive desire in you. Where have you given into excessive desire? It is important to tell God through prayer that you understand that this excessive desire is not his will. Let him know that you understand and agree that this excessive form of this desire is destructive. Agree with him that there must be some other ways to live life that are better and more fulfilling that do not include excessive desires.

If you have embraced an excessive desire, confess to the Lord that you are wrong. Thank him that he has forgiven you in Christ. Ask him to direct and energize you to no longer give into that desire in the future. Move forward in his forgiveness to a better life. The Devil does not want your excessive desire to return to normal because he would lose a level of control over you. He has been turning you away from righteous opportunities by igniting your excessive desire. It is time to fix that and bring your desires back to a normal level.

Look at the following list and prayerfully go through each desire. Ask God if there are any desires that are beyond the normal levels. It is can be very difficult to bring an excessive desire back down to a normal level but through Christ it is possible. In some areas where a person has lived a life of excessive desire, that desire has to be eliminated completely; there is no moderation. If a person is an alcoholic, they cannot moderate their consumption of alcohol; they must eliminate it. This is not always the case, though, so we should just moderate the desire in order to stay on the path of righteousness.

- Pride
- Envy
- Anger
- Lust
- Sloth
- Gluttony
- Greed

The Need for Repentance

When we have embraced an excessive desire, we need to change our mind about that behavior. The word *repentance* is the word for "changing our mind." We used to think it was "okay" to do something or say something or treat people in a certain way, but now we realize that it is wrong. Change your mind about the behavior and head in the opposite direction. Realize that you will have the help to actually act in new ways and not give into excessive desire, but the change of mind is crucial. You must embrace the truth that this excessive desire is not helping you—it is imprisoning you; it is destroying you.

Remember, you will most likely still receive promptings, urges, ideas, and encouragement from others to give in to the temptation in the future. This is where your repentance is crucial. You have decided that you will head in the opposite direction. You have asked God for his power and path. You have said that you would obey when God directs you away from this desire. Follow through...there must be a way to moderate or eliminate this desire. It will often require setting more boundaries and help than you have had in the past, but it is possible. All kinds of people every day stop allowing excessive desire to rule their life. There are all kinds of Christian organizations and even some secular ones that will assist you in a righteous way to get a handle on an excessive desire.

The Need for Protection

Once we agree with God and change our mind, we need to put actual systems, stops, or things in place that will keep us from moving in that direction again. God wants you to begin putting guardrails or fences up so that you can't give in to this temptation any more. What do those look like? Yes, you will feel the pull of that temptation again, so you need to have put fences in place so that you can't sin in that way even if you want to. You may not know how to bring these protections into your life, but someone does. Find the people who have experience with this temptation and listen when they share what they have seen others do and what must be done to defeat this particular test/temptation. Ideally you want to put systems in place so that in a moment of weakness, when you notice you are being led astray, you cannot give in even if you want to.

When you are facing repeated temptations to move beyond the path of righteousness, ask these questions and act to protect yourself against excessive desires. Remember, these desires may be any of the seven deadly sins (pride, envy, anger, lust, sloth, gluttony, greed) or some others. Do not leave the will of God, the path of righteousness; there is nothing out there but heartache. The Devil promises freedom and pleasure, but it is hollow and leads to a form of slavery to sin. He is always leading away from the abundant life God has planned. Don't fall for it.

Exercises to Defeat The Tempter

Deploying the Armor of God

How do we defeat the Devil as he tempts us? There are eight actions and spiritual antidotes that are essential to winning the life God has always wanted for you: the Armor of God (Eph. 6:10-18). They will be a crucial part of beating the temptations of the Devil. He wants to destroy us and add us to his manure pile of wasted people, wasted skills, wasted opportunities, and wasted lives; but we can win the life that God has planned for us through Christ. God has given us all we need; we just have to start using all that he has provided for us.

The spiritual weapons in the Armor of God are truth, righteousness, peace, faith, salvation, the Word of God (God's Wisdom), prayer, and alertness. The Devil acts against these qualities because in order to destroy a life, he needs to distort or attack each of these. In every scheme there is an attack against, or distortion of, one of these spiritual realities. It is these qualities that bring health, blessing, peace, and joy to people.

Let me write these again in a graphically interesting way so you will hopefully remember them. Memorize them. Use them. Write your own copy of them. Draw them. Ask God for insight on how to increase their use in your life. You and I will need these to defeat the Schemes of the Devil.

Truth

   Righteousness

      Peace

         Faith

            Salvation

               Word of God

                  Prayer

                     Alertness

In these we have the answers, the antidotes, and the super-weapons that will defeat the Devil's accusations and deceptions. We also have the Holy Spirit guiding us as to which one to use at what time. Each of these spiritual weapons is a scheme buster, but we are to be guided by the Holy Spirit in our deployment of these weapons. We don't just use all the weapons every time we sense a spiritual attack; there are usually one or two that need our focus at a time. There are numerous examples in Scripture where the Holy Spirit directed people to use only one or two weapons instead of all of them (Matt. 4:1-12; Matt. 26:36-46). When I am under attack, I pray down through these spiritual weapons and ask God to guide me to just the right one for the particular temptation I am facing.

Now it is important to note that the first three spiritual weapons are to be deployed constantly in your life. As the Apostle Paul outlines, these spiritual weapons are distinct between the first three and the last five.

Stand firm therefore, HAVING GIRDED YOUR LOINS WITH TRUTH, and HAVING PUT ON THE BREASTPLATE OF RIGHTEOUSNESS, and having shod YOUR FEET WITH THE PREPARATION OF THE GOSPEL OF PEACE; in addition to all, taking up the shield of faith with which you will be able to extinguish all the flaming arrows of the evil one. And take THE HELMET OF SALVATION, and the sword of the Spirit, which is the word of God. With all prayer and petition pray at all times in the Spirit, and with this in view, be on the alert with all perseverance and petition for all the saints, (Eph. 6:14-18).

Notice that for the first three he uses the past tense verb of *having*, as in already in the past having put on these weapons: Truth, Righteousness, and Peace. You are always to be standing on truth and learning more. We are always to be righteous and loving. We are always to be peaceable and forgiving. The last five weapons are to be taken up and deployed when the battle rages: Faith, Salvation, Word of God, Prayer, and Alertness.

Engaging God in Your Spiritual Battle with the Devil

Just as Jesus was completely dependent upon the Father and the Spirit, we are dependent upon the whole of the Trinity for our victory in the spiritual battles of our life. Too many Christians act like they are on their own when facing the Devil. They think God threw the manual (Bible) at them and told them, "Read it; all the answers are in there." God is with us. He has prepared all the weapons for us to use. He knows the right strategy to use and will give us wisdom and guidance if we ask for it and expect to receive it. Seriously ask God the following questions when you think the Devil is tempting, testing, or scheming against you.

What spiritual weapon should I to use against **excessive desire?**

- Is it truth?
- Is it righteousness?
- Is it peace?
- Is it faith or God-ordained risk?
- Is it a God-provided way of escape or element of hope?
- Is it wisdom from God's Word?
- Is it prayer?
- Is it alertness and precaution?

Once you have answered these questions, then it is time to go deeper into the particular weapon you are supposed to deploy. In the exercises that follow I have made a lot of educated guesses about what you may need to defeat a particular scheme, but it is more important that you stay sensitive to the Lord Jesus as he guides you to the particular way of using the Armor of God to defeat the schemes of Satan. It is also very helpful to have a pastor, mentor, life coach, wise friend, or counselor help you understand how to defeat the enemy. When you are facing excessive desire of one of the deadly sins or something else, act to protect yourself by first asking these questions. You can resist the Devil's siren call in the area of your struggle. God loves us and wants us to get through this test so we can become stronger on the other side. The Devil is always leading away from the abundant life God has planned. Don't fall for it. Run toward God's righteous plans for your life.

Further Questions to Ask

Pray down through these questions and let God the Holy Spirit guide you to the particular spiritual weapon that he wants you to deploy against whichever excessive desire you are facing.

What **truth**(s) would stop this temptation and deliver the individual, group, or nation?

- It may be truths about God that will win the day.
- It may be truths about Christian living that will win the day.
- It may be truths about ourselves that will win the day.
- It may be truths about others and/or society that will win the day.
- It may be a particular scientific fact or historical field that will dispel the deception and schemes of the enemy.

What **righteousness, love, or morality** would stop this temptation and deliver the individual, group, or nation?

- It may be that you need to increase your love in one of the relationships of your life.
- It may be that you need to increase the wisdom of the love in one of your relationships.
- It may be that you need to do good and right things that you have not been doing.

- It may be that you need to stop doing some unloving, unrighteous, or damaging actions or words.
- It may be that you need to ask about an opportunity you are being given:

  • Will this actually do good? Will this harm others?

  • Is this really just about my desire and I am being led along by my desire?

What **peace moves** or strategies would stop this temptation and deliver the individual, group, or nation?

- It may be that you need to make peace with God in ways that you haven't yet.
- It may be that you need to examine or lower your expectations or the anger will still win.
- It may be that you need to change some of your actions or the circumstances that surround the tense moments in your life.
- It may be that you need to forgive God, yourself, or others to defeat this scheme.
- It may be that you need to turn this enemy into a friend.
- It may be that you need to stop acting with hostility in a particular situation.
- It may be that you need to start positive steps to bring about peace with others.
- It may be that you need to leave all justice with God.
- It may be that you need more than just peace; you need harmony with another person.

What **faith steps** or God-directed risks would stop this temptation and deliver the individual, group, or nation?

- It may be that you need to trust God for something that is right but very hard to do.
- It may be that you need to learn more about God and the Christian life so that your trust is more solid and informed.
- It may be that God wants you to trust Him and head in a new direction to defeat this particular scheme of the Devil.
- It may be that you need to decide to trust God when it doesn't feel like the best solution.
- It may be that you must trust God when you are making no progress, as that is better than the progress toward the wrong goals.

What **ways of escape (salvation) or hope** would stop this temptation and deliver the individual, group, or nation?

- It may be that you need to explore and take fuller advantage of the salvation that is in the Lord Jesus Christ than you have in the past.
- It may be that you are supposed to take some way of escape that will get you out of a situation that is too tempting, too pressurized, too dangerous, or too life altering for you.
- It may be that you must hold on to or look for the elements of hope from your past and in the present as you wait for God's deliverance.

- It may be that you have to cling to the hope of your salvation: the return of Christ and your place in heaven to say *no* to the temptations of the Devil in this life.

What **wisdom from God's Word** would stop this temptation and deliver the individual, group, or nation?

- It may be that you need to read the Scriptures daily so that God can prompt you with the appropriate verses when you need them.
- It may be that you need to read through the Scriptures so that you have a grasp of what God is saying in the whole of the Word of God.
- It may be that you need to go to a class, seminar, or small group where you can get a better overview of the Old and New Testament.
- It may be that you need to learn how to study the Scriptures so that when God prompts you with a verse, you can study it and gain the appropriate understanding of what God is saying.
- It may be that you need to learn how to meditate on the Word of God so that when God gives you a Scripture, you know how to carry it around in your mind all day.
- It may be that you need to quote a verse of Scripture to yourself all day to defeat the scheme the Devil is running.
- It may be that you need to quote a particular verse of Scripture at the Devil to let him know that you are on to his scheme. You now know the wisdom of God and will not be fooled by his ideas and opportunities.

What **kind and type of prayers** would stop this temptation and deliver the individual, group, or nation?

- It may be that God prompts you to spend time praising Him as the antidote to a particular scheme of the Devil.
- It may be that God wants you to prayerfully contemplate a Scripture as the way to win against a particular scheme.
- It may be that God wants you to request certain things from Him that you will need to win against this particular scheme.
- It may be that God wants you to pray for someone else to defeat this scheme.
- It may be that you need to pray prayers of gratefulness in order to pass the test that is being thrown at you.
- It may be that you need to confess your sins or the sins of the group or your nation in order to stop this scheme from succeeding.
- It may be that God wants you to battle for the unconverted soul(s) you know that need the Lord in order to defeat this particular scheme of the Devil.
- It may be that you need to pray for government officials that they would be safe and ethical as they make decisions that are unthreatened by interests groups that are evil.

What **precautions and/or alertness** would stop this temptation and deliver the individual, group, or nation?

- It may be that God wants you to make very specific preparations to withstand a scheme or test of the Devil.
- It may be that you have an exposed weakness to sin that will damage, dishonor, or destroy you if it is not dealt

with, and you must protect yourself and your loved ones in some way before the storm of the test arrives.

- It may be that you do not know enough about a crucial relationship or truth of Christianity and God is giving you the heads-up about learning how to make that right. You must act before the test comes, or it will hurt you or stop your progress.

Scheme #2

The Devil Scheme

(Amplified Lies and Accusations)

Mary was a bright, attractive, and engaging young woman; but she had a propensity to play the victim. Slowly but surely over many years she became increasingly comfortable being the victim which meant that other people then had to be the bad people. Eventually there were no misunderstandings in her world; there was only more evidence that most people were out to get her. When she went into victim-mode she cursed, yelled, was vindictive, manipulative, and spewed out lies. She increasingly fell under the spell of what I call, *the Devil Scheme (Amplified Lies and Accusations)*. This scheme is where the Devil and his demons attack a person with accusations, lies, and a delusional world. In Mary's case it was so sad because she did not want to come back to the real world where people make mistakes and where her friends and family really loved her. No, she wanted to see everything in black or white. You were either agreeing with her that she was a victim or you were an oppressor.

Another example of a person falling under the Devil Scheme is the case of Jim. Jim was a very talented and dynamic young man, but he increasingly came under the sway of internal accusations and depression that he was not perfect. Even though he had lots of things going for him, he couldn't seem to shake the pessimism that he allowed to settle in on his mind. Eventually Jim gave into this melancholy orientation and tried to take his own life. He did not succeed, but it created another accusation and another mental failure that pummeled him. Now, it is not true that all depression comes from the Devil but some does. There are chemical, situational, emotional, and other sources for depression and pessimism; but there are also spiritual causes and these can occur when Satan runs The *Devil Scheme*.

This scheme is so common that many people do not recognize it as foreign to them. They have allowed their minds to be warped to the point where the negative bent -- the deception that they are living under -- is normal and the accepted way of operating. The constant feeling of condemnation, accusation, and inadequacy is normal for them. It is actually not normal, but is often a result of the Devil running a scheme against us to hold us down and keep us from becoming what we truly could become.

The word *Devil* is from the Greek word *diabolos*, which means "slanderer, accuser." There is also in this word and its use in the New Testament the idea of "deceiver." The deception is to get you to accept the accusation or trap. The Devil will weave an elaborate deception to get you to stop doing righteousness and to do something else. In the guise of a serpent, the Devil wove an elaborate series of questions to Eve so he could make one accusation against God, namely that God was holding back the good stuff from her and her husband, Adam. Unfortunately she embraced the deception and the accusation and plunged the whole world into sin (Gen. 3:1-7). This scheme that Lucifer will run against us is about slander, lies, accusation, gossip, and rumor...all wrapped in deception.

I am working with a married couple where the young lady sees herself as the victim. No matter what great lengths her husband goes through to demonstrate his love for her and the family, she wants, and even needs, to be the victim in the relationship. His efforts are never enough or right. Her mind has embraced the Devil's accusations about her husband. He needs to be the bad guy, and so her mind examines every aspect of his life in such a way as to make him the bad guy. She sees him as horrible even though he is one of the most giving, kind, and faithful husbands I have ever worked with. She will most likely destroy her marriage because she has believed the deception and the accusations. Just as a word of warning: if the wise people in your life all see your situation different than you see it, realize that you are probably being deceived in some way. The collective wisdom of wise people should be embraced.

Some of the most ruthless and difficult attacks to fend off are these deceptive internal accusations that come through thoughts, perspectives, and emotions. The Devil is famous for pounding us with how unworthy we are or someone else is. He can deceive people into believing that our loved ones will be better off if we committed suicide. He pounds us with how guilty we are for what we have done. When he is running *The Accusation and Deception Scheme,* the attacks may come from others or they may be entirely internal. Remember, the Devil can put thoughts in our mind that are not our thoughts (John 13:2). But we can resist these accusations and lies and embrace truth instead. God is clear in Romans 8:1,

> *There is therefore no condemnation for those who are in Christ Jesus.*

The condemnation is not coming from God. It is coming from the Devil and his associates. God will bring conviction and wants us to repent, but he will not hammer us and suggest harming ourselves as a way of helping.

The Devil Scheme (Amplified Lies and Accusations) mostly involves infections of the soul and spirit. Lucifer's weapons are lies, bitterness, discouragement, pessimism, depression, fear, slander, accusation, and hopelessness. He is attacking the source of your hope and seeking to infect it with a disease that will sap your strength and make everything seem too hard and too complex. If you lose your hope, then you will fall for almost anything. One famous pastor says that his number one job each day is to stay encouraged and positive. Just like a cold or fever causes a person to climb in bed and view regular life as too hard, so infections of the soul and spirit make the regular elements of life seem too hard. Realize that the Devil does not want you to cooperate with God to accomplish anything big, so he wants you to be too discouraged to become a partner with God. This scheme is so common that we don't see it clearly. We view our negativity as normal. It takes work to stay positive. It is not normal to be under a cloud of negative, condemning thinking. If this sounds familiar to you, it may suggest that Satan is running this scheme against you.

Related Scriptures

1 Peter 5:8 - *Be of sober spirit, be on the alert. Your adversary, the Devil, prowls around like a roaring lion, seeking someone to devour.*

A part of this scheme is to devour you with accusation, deception, gossip, pride, and so forth. The Devil's goal is to no longer have you make progress along the road of righteousness. There is some good work that you are supposed to do, and the Devil wants to derail you doing that in some way (Eph. 2:10). He may send a false accusation. He may weave an elaborate deception based on bogus facts. For example, we know that the scientist, Ernest Hackel, doctored the embryonic stages of development to prove the macro evolutionary case that ended up destroying belief in God for many people who gave up their faith based upon those drawings that were in their textbook. The Devil could use a rumor that makes others doubt your character or ability or love. How many distraught husbands fall victim to a lie, a deception, or a rumor and kill their children, their wife, and themselves because they think that they will never get to see their kids again or they will be bankrupt. The Devil could use an internal accusation that all of a sudden pops up in your mind. It could be a mocking word from someone you know. It could be a formal investigation of your finances or work history. He wants you to stop doing what you are doing, and so he runs this scheme as a way to bring your good works to a halt. Resist him. Keep making progress for the good.

Luke 4:2, 3 - *For forty days, being tempted by the Devil. And He ate nothing during those days, and when they had ended, He became hungry. And the Devil said to Him, "If You are the Son of God, tell this stone to become bread."*

Notice how this interaction between Jesus and the Devil goes. It is really at the heart an accusation: If you are the Son of God, prove it. The Devil wants Jesus to use his own deity to live this human life and thereby disqualify himself as the perfect man. Jesus does not respond to the accusation but instead reiterates his dependence upon the Father and the Word of God. Jesus is clearly hungry after a forty-day fast, but he sees the real intent of the Devil's scheme. It is an accusation to get Jesus to act in a way that will move him out of the will of God for his life here on earth. If Jesus were to respond and turn the stones into bread using his own deity, then he would no longer be the perfect man, the second

Adam, who could win a way back to God for humanity through his perfect sacrifice. Jesus could clearly have turned the stones into bread.

Luke 8:12 - *Those beside the road are those who have heard; then the Devil comes and takes away the word from their heart, so that they will not believe and be saved.*

This is a verse from the Parable of the Sower. Jesus is saying that there are four kinds of people in their interaction with the good news of God's forgiveness. One of the types is the person who is so hardened because of the Devil's accusations and deceptions that the good news bounces off their heart and they can't even engage with God's forgiveness. The Devil has run *The Accusation and Deception Scheme* so long and so well that it has been thoroughly embraced. This kind of person does not believe that they are worthy to be forgiven. This kind of person suspects that God is not a good God. This kind of person may have fixated on a negative experience in a church and because of that has written off God, Jesus, forgiveness, and eternal life. Some of these types of people believe that they are too far gone to help. They have believed the lies that others have said about them. In some way they have hardened their heart against the work of God. The Scriptures tell us that the Devil has a hand in the good news bouncing off their soul.

Lucifer has been running this scheme for thousands of years on people to beat them down and destroy their ability to embrace the wonder of God and his love for them. We all see evidence of people who have embraced this scheme. Let me give you just one more example. I have often wondered how a person would get to the place where they would have tattooed on their body: "Born to Lose." *The Devil Scheme* is how a person gets to this place where this makes sense to them. They have been attacked so often about their unworthiness that they have mentally embraced that they will always lose in every negotiation, and they think that they deserve it. It is this kind of person that I want to give The Good News. You are not born to lose. You can choose. You can change the trajectory of your life. God will forgive. God will empower.

John 13:2 - *During supper, the Devil having already put into the heart of Judas Iscariot, the son of Simon, to betray Him,*

Notice that the Devil put in the heart of Judas to betray Jesus. Judas did not have to listen to the thoughts and ideas of the Devil, but he did. Somehow the Devil put a thought in Judas' mind so that betraying Jesus sounded like the logical thing to do. It was all deception and lies, but it sounded right. There are various theories as to what type of thoughts Satan had to put in Judas' mind to get him to do this. Some have suggested that Jesus increasingly disappointed Judas by his unwillingness to be made king and fight the Romans. Others have suggested that Satan pointed out how Jesus' allowing Mary to anoint Jesus with the expensive bottle of perfume kept Judas from skimming off the thirty pieces of silver he would have pocketed normally with these kinds of donations. Whatever the Devil dropped in Judas' mind, he did such a good job of accusing Jesus that Judas was willing to betray him to the Jewish authorities. Judas believed these thoughts were coming from him, but they were really coming from the Devil; and Judas was running with them. The infection of soul and spirit pervaded Judas until he did the unthinkable; he betrayed the Son of God. He woke up from his infection after he had done the deed and was immediately set upon by the Devil again with new accusations, and he killed himself.

Do not fall victim to this scheme. It will often require help from friends, counselors, and mentors to resist this powerful scheme; but it is essential that you find a way to win against this strategy of the Devil. Realize that all the thoughts that go through your mind may not be your own. Stay grounded to reality and do not embrace deception. If everybody is telling you that you are deceived in what you are thinking or doing, then listen. You are Christ's son or daughter. You have been bought with a price. You are not valuable because you can do something. Your intrinsic value is yours as an image bearer of God (Gen. 1:26).

Ephesians 4:26, 27 - *Be angry, and yet do not sin; do not let the sun go down on your anger, and do not give the Devil an opportunity.*

This is a very important verse that tells us that repeated sin allows the Devil to gain a foothold or an opportunity to wreak havoc in our life. He wants to weave a deception and land an accusation against your spouse, against God, and against you so that you will act in ways that destroy the very things that you love the most. In this particular section of Scripture, God is talking about anger and why it should be resolved. If we get angry and do not resolve it in our soul, then the Devil can have an opportunity in our lives. The actual Greek word is *topas* or "place." The Devil is looking for a beachhead in our lives so that he can weave his deceptions and accusations. He wants the good work we are doing in our marriage, as a parent, or as a Christian stopped; and he is seeing if you will fall for his deception.

2 Timothy 2:26 - *...and they may come to their senses and escape from the snare of the Devil, having been held captive by him to do his will.*

This verse of Scripture tells us plainly that it is possible to be so deceived by Lucifer when he is running this scheme on us that we do not have our normal mental faculty and can be held captive by him to do the Devil's will. The deception and the accusations are so strong that they tend to control how we act. Haven't we all seen people who go deep down the rabbit hole in this or that conspiracy theory that seems to make sense, but it involves selling things and giving the proceeds to some organization. I know of people who willingly leave their families and surrender their lives over to a commune or cult. These are extreme cases and the Devil has much more nuanced deceptions also. I know people who give themselves over to making money and every dollar they make is a good thing no matter how they have to make it. I know people who need to express their anger and rage even though it destroys every hope of a normal life and normal relationships. These are all snares of *The Devil Scheme.*

Ultimately, this scheme is all about the Devil testing your ability to handle being accused. This means that he will use other people to accuse you and mentally plant accusations in your mind. He will put you under investigation. He will hope that you will crack and cheat to get out from the accusation or do something else stupid to make the accusers have something to look at.

A common way that Lucifer gets you to stop doing righteous things is by bringing an accusation against you about something you did in the past or he starts a rumor about you so that you will back off and stop the good work you are starting.

Have you suffered under this scheme of accusation, lies, doubt, and deception?

Exercises to Defeat The Devil

How do we defeat the Devil as he accuses and deceives us? There are eight actions and spiritual antidotes that are known as the Armor of God that are essential to winning the life God has always wanted for you. They will be a crucial part of beating the temptations of the Devil. The Devil wants to destroy us and add us to his manure pile of wasted people, wasted skills, wasted opportunities, and wasted lives. But we can win the life that God has planned for us through Christ. God has given us all we need; we just have to start using all that he has provided.

These spiritual weapons are truth, righteousness, peace, faith, salvation, the Word of God (God's Wisdom), prayer, and alertness. The Devil acts against these qualities because in order to destroy a life, he needs to distort or attack each of these. In every scheme there is an attack against, or distortion of, one of these spiritual realities. It is these qualities that bring health, blessing, peace, and joy to people.

Let me write these again in a graphically interesting way so you will hopefully remember them. Memorize them. Use them. Write your own copy of them. Draw them. Ask God for insight on how to increase their use in your life. You and I will need these to defeat the Schemes of the Devil.

Truth

Righteousness

Peace

Faith

Salvation

Word of God

Prayer

Alertness

In these we have the answers, the antidotes, and the super-weapons that will defeat the Devil's accusations and deceptions. We also have the Holy Spirit guiding us as to which one to use at what time. Each of these spiritual weapons is a scheme buster, but we are to be guided by the Holy Spirit in our deployment of these weapons. We don't just use all the weapons every time we sense a spiritual attack; there are usually one or two that need our focus at a time. There are numerous examples in Scripture where the Holy Spirit directed people to use only one or two weapons instead of all of them (Matt. 4:1-12; Matt. 26:36-46). When I am under attack, I pray down through these spiritual weapons and ask God to guide me to just the right one for the particular temptation I am facing.

Now it is important to note that the first three spiritual weapons are to be deployed constantly in your life. As the Apostle Paul outlines, these spiritual weapons are distinct between the first three and the last five.

Stand firm therefore, <u>HAVING</u> GIRDED YOUR LOINS WITH TRUTH, and <u>HAVING</u> PUT ON THE BREASTPLATE OF RIGHTEOUSNESS, and <u>having</u> shod YOUR FEET WITH THE PREPARATION OF THE GOSPEL OF

PEACE; in addition to all, taking up the shield of faith with which you will be able to extinguish all the flaming arrows of the evil one. And take THE HELMET OF SALVATION, and the sword of the Spirit, which is the word of God. With all prayer and petition pray at all times in the Spirit, and with this in view, be on the alert with all perseverance and petition for all the saints... (Eph. 6:14-18)

Notice that for the first three, he uses the past tense verb *of having,* as in already in the past having put on these weapons: Truth, Righteousness, and Peace. You are always to be standing on truth and learning more. We are always to be righteous and loving. We are always to be peaceable and forgiving. The last five weapons are to be taken up and deployed when the battle rages: Faith, Salvation, Word of God, Prayer, and Alertness.

Engaging God in Your Spiritual Battle with the Devil

Just as Jesus was completely dependent upon the Father and the Spirit, we are dependent upon the whole of the Trinity for our victory in the spiritual battles of our life. Too many Christians act like they are on their own when facing the Devil. They think God threw the manual (Bible) at them and told them, "Read it; all the answers are in there." God is with us and has prepared all the weapons, knows the right strategy, and will give us wisdom and guidance if we ask for it and expect to receive it. Seriously ask God the following questions when you think the Devil is tempting, testing, or scheming against you.

What spiritual weapon should I to use against **accusation, lies, and deception?**

- Is it truth?
- Is it righteousness?
- Is it peace?
- Is it faith or God-ordained risk?
- Is it a God-provided way of escape or element of hope?
- Is it wisdom from God's Word?
- Is it prayer?
- Is it alertness and precaution?

Once you have answered these questions, then it is time to go deeper on the particular weapons you are supposed to deploy. In the exercises that follow I have made a lot of educated guesses about what you may need to defeat a particular scheme, but it is more important that you stay sensitive to the Lord Jesus as he guides you to the particular way of using the Armor of God to defeat the schemes of Satan. It is also very helpful to have a pastor, mentor, life coach, wise friend, or counselor help you understand how to defeat the enemy. When you are facing repeated accusations from others internally, ask these questions and act to protect yourself. The Devil's accusations, lies, and deception are not real. God loves us and wants us to get through this test and be stronger on the other side. If it sounds too good to be true, it probably is. If everybody else is saying that this group or theory is wrong, then it has a chance of being wrong. The Devil is always leading away from the abundant life God has planned. Don't fall for it.

Further Questions to Ask

Pray down through these questions and let God the Holy Spirit guide you to the particular spiritual weapon that he wants you to deploy against these accusations, lies, or deceptions you are facing.

What **truth(s)** would stop these **accusations, lies, or deceptions** and deliver the individual, group, or nation?

- It may be truths about God that will win the day.
- It may be truths about Christian living that will win the day.
- It may be truths about ourselves that will win the day.
- It may be truths about others and/or society that will win the day.
- It may be a particular scientific fact or historical field that will dispel the deception and schemes of the enemy.

What **righteousness, love, or morality** would stop these **accusations, lies, or deceptions** and deliver the individual, group, or nation?

- It may be that you need to increase your love in one of the relationships of your life.
- It may be that you need to increase the wisdom of the love in one of your relationships.
- It may be that you need to do good and right things that you have not been doing.
- It may be that you need to stop doing some unloving, unrighteous, or damaging actions or words.

- It may be that you need to ask about an opportunity you are being given:
  • Will this actually do good? Will this harm others?
  • Is this really just about my desire and I am being led along by my desire?

What **peace moves** or strategies would stop these **accusations, lies, or deceptions** and deliver the individual, group, or nation?

- It may be that you need to make peace with God in ways that you haven't yet.
- It may be that you need to examine or lower your expectations or the anger will still win.
- It may be that you need to change some of your actions or the circumstances that surround the tense moments in your life.
- It may be that you need to forgive God, yourself, or others to defeat this scheme.
- It may be that you need to turn this enemy into a friend.
- It may be that you need to stop acting with hostility in a particular situation.
- It may be that you need to start positive steps to bring about peace with others.
- It may be that you need to leave all justice with God.
- It may be that you need more than just peace; you need harmony with another person.

What **faith steps** or God-directed risks would stop these **accusations, lies, or deceptions** and deliver the individual, group, or nation?

- It may be that you need to trust God for something that is right but very hard to do.
- It may be that you need to learn more about God and the Christian life so that your trust is more solid and informed.
- It may be that God wants you to trust him and head in a new direction to defeat this particular scheme of the Devil.
- It may be that you need to decide to trust God when it doesn't feel like the best solution.
- It may be that you must trust God when you are making no progress as that is better than the progress toward the wrong goals.

What **ways of escape (salvation) or hope** would stop these **accusations, lies, or deceptions** and deliver the individual, group, or nation?

- It may be that you need to explore and take fuller advantage of the salvation that is in the Lord Jesus Christ than you have in the past.
- It may be that you are supposed to take some way of escape that will get you out of a situation that is too tempting, too pressurized, too dangerous, or too life altering for you.
- It may be that you must hold on to or look for the elements of hope from your past and in the present as you wait for God's deliverance.

- It may be that you have to cling to the hope of your salvation: the return of Christ and your place in heaven to say *no* to the temptations of the Devil in this life.

What **wisdom from God's Word** would stop these **accusations, lies, or deceptions** and deliver the individual, group, or nation?

- It may be that you need to read the Scriptures daily so that God can prompt you with the appropriate verses when you need them.
- It may be that you need to read through the Scriptures so that you have a grasp of what God is saying in the whole of the Word of God.
- It may be that you need to go to a class, seminar, or small group where you can get a better overview of the Old and New Testament.
- It may be that you need to learn how to study the Scriptures so that when God prompts you with a verse, you can study it and gain the appropriate understanding of what God is saying.
- It may be that you need to learn how to meditate on the Word of God so that when God gives you a Scriptures, you know how to carry it around in your mind all day.
- It may be that you need to quote a verse of Scripture to yourself all day to defeat the scheme the Devil is running.
- It may be that you need to quote a particular verse of Scripture at the Devil to let him know that you are on to his scheme. You now know the wisdom of God and will not be fooled by his ideas and opportunities.

What **kind and type of prayers** would stop these **accusations, lies, or deceptions** and deliver the individual, group, or nation?

- It may be that God prompts you to spend time praising him as the antidote to a particular scheme of the Devil.
- It may be that God wants you to prayerfully contemplate a Scripture as the way to win against a particular scheme.
- It may be that God wants you to request certain things from him that you will need to win against this particular scheme.
- It may be that God wants you to pray for someone else to defeat this scheme.
- It may be that you need to pray prayers of gratefulness in order to pass the test that is being thrown at you.
- It may be that you need to confess your sins or the sins of the group or your nation in order to stop this scheme from succeeding.
- It may be that God wants you to battle for the unconverted soul(s) you know that need the Lord in order to defeat this particular scheme of the Devil.
- It may be that you need to pray for government officials that they would be safe and ethical as they make decisions, unthreatened by interests groups that are evil.

What **precautions and/or alertness** would stop these **accusations, lies, or deceptions** and deliver the individual, group, or nation?

- It may be that God wants you to make very specific preparations to withstand a scheme or test of the Devil.

- It may be that you have an exposed weakness to sin that will damage, dishonor, or destroy you if it is not dealt with; and you must protect yourself and your loved ones in some way before the storm of the test arrives.
- It may be that you do not know enough about a crucial relationship or truth of Christianity, and God is giving you the heads-up about learning how to make that right. You must act before the test comes, or it will hurt you or stop your progress.

Scheme #3

The Satan Scheme
(Amplified Opposition)

I had a conversation the other day with a man we will call Gideon. He described working for a boss who honestly thought he was a very good boss; but he was really deeply selfish, rude, destructive, and demeaning to the people and the company where they all worked. Here is how Gideon described his feelings as he had a meeting with his old boss after he had left the company:

> I met with an enemy the other day and he had no clue how much pain, anguish, and disruption he caused. Randy (my boss) was just living his life, thinking his actions were a blessing to me. He has no idea how he disrespected me; how humiliated he made me feel on numerous occasions; how he constantly blocked good things from happening in the company. He does not realize how his selfishness destroyed so many good things that were beginning to happen. Randy's constant self-focus sucked the energy out of the rooms he entered. He is totally unprepared to hear what he did to me, to the

other people who worked for him, and to the company. He would be offended if I told him. His defense would be that that was not his intent. His true intent was always: What do I like; what will make me look good; what do I think should be done? His intent was not what is in the best interest of the company; what is in the best interest of that other person; what are other ideas better than my own? He believes that he was my benefactor and the organization's savior, not its destroyer. As I sat there the other day talking with him, I felt a mixture of deep pain for what he had done to me and pity for his complete lack of understanding of all he did.

Gideon and I discussed that his former boss (Randy) had no idea that he was the channel for *The Satan Scheme* to enter the company where they both worked. By Randy's unwillingness to accept honest and clear feedback, he stayed self-focused. This boss is an exemplar for hundreds of spouses, children, parents, bosses, colleagues, and even friends who are clueless to the damage they cause. This person becomes our enemy because they step on everything good we try and do and disrespect our person and work—all because they listen to the whispers of Satan scheming in their souls. All of us can become the channel for *The Satan Scheme* to be run against someone. Oftentimes only honest loving feedback will wake us up to the truth of what we're doing. This is the same situation that the Apostle Peter ran into when he opposed Jesus going to the cross in Matthew 16:22,23.

The Satan Scheme is a major scheme that the Devil will use against us. The word *Satan* is a literal transliteration of the

Hebrew word spelled s-a-t-a-n. The meaning of this word is "opponent, adversary, enemy." God gives this being called Satan (Lucifer) the titles of Opponent, Adversary, and Enemy for a reason. All of us will face opposition in our life, and it is not all from Satan. But there are times when what we are getting is the Devil and his demons running this scheme of opposition against us. He wants us to stop something that we are doing. When the Devil comes in the guise as Satan, he or the person through whom he is running the scheme becomes our adversary.

Internal and External Opposition

In this scheme -- as in all other schemes -- Satan can come against righteous progress through internal or external opposition. If he is running an internal scheme, then he wants you to become your own enemy. He wants to convince you mentally, emotionally, or spiritually to stop something you are doing. Remember, internal opposition is made up of thoughts, feelings, willfulness, and attitudes sent to overwhelm, distract, or dissuade us from a righteous path. External opposition comes through friends, officials, enemies, institutions, and even governments. It is normal to have some level of opposition or pushback when one starts new initiatives; but when Satan runs *The Satan Scheme*, the level of opposition is at a whole new level. Just because there is a little resistance to what you want to do doesn't mean it is Satan. But if there is an almost overwhelming internal or external resistance to what God is asking you to do, then you are most likely facing this oppositional scheme. This is where you must stand firm and resist. Do not be shoved back. Do not quit.

Whenever we are making progress in righteousness, this is when he wants to oppose our progress. Many times when we are serving God the most powerfully, Satan comes to test that progress as our Adversary. He runs an oppositional scheme against us and almost dares us to trust God over the internal and external opposition we are getting. If whenever any of us think of doing something noble, good, stretching, or big and we immediately think of concerns, reasons, and obstacles why we should not do this good thing, it might be this oppositional scheme being run against us. The Devil and his demons come and amplify those stops and roadblocks in our thinking so we never get started. If we actually do get started doing a good work, then he may persist by running the same "this will never work" thoughts and imaginary obstacles to get us to stop. If we persevere, he may find an external enemy to actually oppose us as the good work becomes public. An external opposition scheme finds a friend, boss, colleague, child, or spouse to oppose your good idea or to throw cold water on it so you won't keep going. It doesn't matter to the Devil who he gets to become our opponent; just so that we are opposed.

There is also another type of scheme that is more open -- a deeper version of *The Satan Scheme*. It is one that is more hostile and being run openly and powerfully against you by someone who is antagonistic toward you. In Matthew 13:39, the Devil is called the *enemy*. This is the word *exthros,* meaning one who is at enmity with another. This person really does want to do harm toward the other. Knowing of this antagonism, the Devil ramps up opposition through a person who really does want harm to come to you. This person becomes your enemy. They really do dislike you. They want to injure, stop, or destroy you. This is not that situation where a person is just going about their business and if you get in their way then "So sorry, but I wanted what I

68

wanted." This is an individual who is pointedly aimed at stopping, injuring, or destroying the other person and their progress, like Alexander the coppersmith, who opposed Paul (2 Tim. 4:14-15). In this scheme, the Devil or a particular demon runs a test by having a particular person be opposed to you at a number of points. This person is not mean to everyone but to you specifically. They are opposed to your righteous progress. They really do not want you to make progress or gain recognition. If it should come to you, then they want to make sure you don't get it. This person is vocally opposed to you and has the power to stop you in a number of ways either legally, physically, corporately, or civically.

Another good example of this version of *The Satan Scheme* is a story about a woman I will call Mary. She was a teacher in the elementary school where I started a church. Mary did everything she could to oppose and hinder our work as a church. She left our piano out in the rain; she hid the sound equipment; and she rallied teachers to be against the church. In every way she could, she threw roadblocks and hindrances to the survivability of our little church. I remember how hard it was and how constantly things were missing or broken and how hostile the mood at the school was. I knew that *The Satan Scheme* was being run against us, but I didn't know how deep it went or who the real ringleader (enemy) of our opposition was until much later. Fortunately the scheme didn't work and our church survived and thrived.

Years later Mary, this openly hostile teacher, wandered into another church in another city and gave her life to Jesus Christ as Savior. Then a few years after that she came back and apologized for all the awful, underhanded things she had done to try and destroy our church. Only then did I become aware of the depth of her involvement in *The Satan Scheme*.

Of course I forgave her and was excited that she was a part of God's forever family. But it was shocking to hear of all the things that she and others had done to oppose our church. God's grace was more than sufficient to sustain the church and eventually allowed it to triumph in that community. And it was sufficient to continue to chase after this woman and embrace her with love and forgiveness.

Look at this Scriptural example of *The Satan Scheme* being run against Israel through King David.

> *Then Satan stood up against Israel and moved David to number Israel. (1 Chron. 21:1)*

The Scriptures show us Satan running *The Satan Scheme* against Israel and he used King David to be the one to run it. David gave into promptings to do what he knew he should not do. When he gave the orders to number the people, his general told him it was not a good idea. But David was swept along in the scheme by following whatever was going through his mind at the time. David made a choice to go along with the internal thoughts, ideas, and attitudes that the Devil was feeding him. And he ignored the feedback he was getting about how wrong this was.

One of our heroes in the Bible fell victim to being a part of Satan's scheme to harm the nation that he loved. This tells us what Satan is capable of doing internally. He convinced King David, a man after God's own heart, to violate God's command and move in league with the Devil to harm his country. If we are not alert, we too will be tempted to do this to the people we love. We may find a person who is a trusted, wise friend being a part of *The Satan Scheme* to oppose something really good that we want to do. Realize we also can be a part of an oppositional scheme against someone else if we are not careful.

Another biblical example of when Satan ran his oppositional scheme was through Judas.

> *And Satan entered into Judas who was called Iscariot belonging to the twelve. And he went away and discussed with the chief priests and officers how he might betray Him to them. (Luke 22:3-4)*

Look at what is said here about how Satan worked with Judas. Satan ran an internal scheme against Judas by entering his mind so that he would become the opposition (enemy, adversary) of Christ. He did not have to give into these thoughts, ideas, attitudes, and emotions that swirled in his head. In fact, he should have known that these bizarre thoughts were hijacking his rational mind. But he allowed his rational self to be completely overwhelmed by this nonsensical scheme, and he became the most hated man in history.

You always have a choice to refute the thoughts in your mind. You don't always have to be the one who does something stupid. You don't have to give in to the adversarial ideas in your head. Jesus said in another part of the gospels that it was inevitable that stumbling blocks would come, but woe to the one through whom they come. In other words, it may be inevitable that something bad will happen; but it doesn't have to happen through you. Judas didn't have to be the betrayer of Christ. He allowed himself to be overwhelmed with a satanic scheme to oppose Christ. Whatever he thought he would gain (thirty pieces of silver) was exposed as toxic because of the deed he did. If you ever find yourself involved in opposing good, no matter how you got there and no matter what it costs to stop, STOP before you go too far. Judas went too far and woke up after the deed had been done. Tragically, Lucifer then ran *The Tempter Scheme* against him until he committed suicide.

Satan ran another oppositional scheme; this time against Peter.

Simon, Simon behold, Satan has demanded permission to sift you like wheat; but I have prayed for you, that your faith may not fail; and you when you have turned again, strengthen your brothers. (Luke 22:31,32)

In the same time period that Judas became convinced to oppose the Lord Jesus, Satan was running *The Satan Scheme* against Peter as we see in his deed of denying Jesus in the courtyard. We see this fascinating glimpse in the way that heaven works in this scenario. Satan got a pre-play of what was going to happen at the arrest of Jesus; and because of what he saw Peter do, he demanded to sift Peter like wheat. Satan was preparing a devastating oppositional scheme against Peter that he would personally run. Jesus does not tell Satan that he cannot run the scheme against Peter; instead Jesus prays for Peter's strength and refining through the process. Lucifer as Satan wanted to destroy Peter and then accuse him like he did with Judas, hoping Peter would also commit suicide and the leadership of the early church would be destroyed. But Jesus prays grace, strength, mercy, and hope into Peter's life. Jesus' prayer wins. Granted, Peter should not have denied Christ but Peter is a better man for the episode.

Related Scriptures

Take a look at these verses where the name *Satan* is used and see the resistance and adversarial nature of what Satan does and how the scheme of opposition works. Remember, the title for Lucifer that is used in the Scripture passage is an indication of the scheme that he is using.

2 Corinthians 12:7 - *Because of the surpassing greatness of the revelations, for this reason, to keep me from exalting myself, there was given me a thorn in the flesh, a messenger of Satan to torment me—to keep me from exalting myself!*

The Apostle Paul tells us that he received incredibly exalted revelations about heaven, Jesus, salvation, and the life hereafter. And because of these revelations, there was a tendency for the Apostle to think too highly of himself. So God allowed a demon to constantly run an oppositional scheme against Paul to keep him humble. The Apostle prayed that he would be healed from this opposing spirit but God said, "No." It was there for a purpose. Imagine what Paul must have thought: "I have abilities as an apostle to heal others and cast our demons, but I cannot throw out this junior demon because God is allowing it to be there to protect me from pride." Paul was better off asking for the extra grace to keep pressing forward, rather than not having the messenger of Satan in his life.

1 Thessalonians 2:18 - *For we wanted to come to you—I, Paul, more than once—and yet Satan hindered us.*

The Scriptures are clear that *The Satan Scheme* is one of adversarial hindrance. This particular Scripture tells us that the Apostle Paul tried to get to the Thessalonian church on more than one occasion but was stopped. Paul knew that his not getting there was because of the Devil and his demons running this scheme.

Be ready for Satan to run *The Satan Scheme* against you. Also be ready to have him enlist you as a participant in the scheme against other people. Don't fall for either of these. Now it is important that we are willing to oppose evil but not in a way that defames the name of Christ.

2 Corinthians 11:14,15 - *No wonder, for even **Satan** disguises himself as an angel of light. Therefore it is not surprising if his servants also disguise themselves as servants of righteousness, whose end will be according to their deeds.*

In this Scripture the Apostle Paul is helping us understand that Satan will at times run *The Satan Scheme* by showing an angelic presence and in that way try and stop some righteous actions or the planning of them. This scheme has a number of ways it can be carried out, but its central issue is opposition and hindrance. Look for these things when you are trying to do something righteous. If you are experiencing opposition and hindrance, then you will probably have uncovered what Satan is up to.

2 Thessalonians 2:9 - *...that is, the one whose coming is in accord with the activity of **Satan**, with all power and signs and false wonders,*

This Scripture tells us that at times *The Satan Scheme* comes with great spiritual power and signs and false wonders. Do not be fooled by spiritual power. If it is aimed at stopping righteous action, it is evil and not good. In every era down through history there have been false revivals and false signs to oppose the real work of God in some area or region. Sometimes when God is doing a great work, the Devil will ratchet up a whole new level of spiritual phenomena to try and confuse people. Sometimes when the gospel penetrates an area, the old spiritual powers are roused to put up a powerful defense of their control. This will take place at extreme levels at the end of history, right before the return of Christ.

So let me sum up here a little bit. *The Satan Scheme* is one of hindrance, opposition, and enemies; and it is designed to stop love, righteousness, God's will, and worship of our great God. Do not be fooled. Also, do not be a part of an oppositional scheme against another person. If the other person is doing righteousness and truly loving things, don't oppose it. Be open to feedback which may tell you that you are going down the wrong track. I hope you realize how subtle Satan is in running this scheme. You can get all caught up in it without realizing that it is really the Devil and his demons and not the flesh and blood people who are irritating you so much. This is what the Apostle Paul says in Eph. 6:12,

> *For our struggle is not against flesh and blood, but against the rulers, against the powers, against the world forces of this darkness, against the spiritual forces of wickedness in the heavenly places.*

The True Opponent

Who does Satan really oppose? You might find it interesting that Satan does not oppose God Himself. He tried that and was judged for that sin (Ezek. 28:12-19; Isa. 14:12-14).[1] Satan is not operating a secret rebel group, which opposes God and aims to overthrow him. Biblically, it is clear that the real target of his opposition is mankind and the holy

---

[1] For a fuller treatment of this issue, read *Satan and the Origin of Evil*, PTLB Publications.

angels. God is using Lucifer's corrupted nature that is now opposed to righteousness to strengthen, deepen, and test our loyalty to righteousness. Lucifer wants to oppose every movement toward righteousness in any place at any time; but God limits the amount, duration, and impact of Satan's opposition. Notice the first chapter of Job and this incredibly powerful oppositional scheme that God allows Lucifer to run against Job in Job 1:1-22.

> *There was a man in the land of Uz whose name was Job; and that man was blameless, upright, fearing God and turning away from evil. Seven sons and three daughters were born to him. His possessions also were 7,000 sheep, 3,000 camels, 500 yoke of oxen, 500 female donkeys, and very many servants; and that man was the greatest of all the men of the east. His sons used to go and hold a feast in the house of each one on his day, and they would send and invite their three sisters to eat and drink with them. When the days of feasting had completed their cycle, Job would send and consecrate them, rising up early in the morning and offering burnt offerings according to the number of them all; for Job said, "Perhaps my sons have sinned and cursed God in their hearts."*
> *Thus Job did continually. Now there was a day when the sons of God came to present themselves before the LORD, and **Satan** also came among them. The LORD said to **Satan**, "From where do you come?" Then **Satan** answered the LORD and said, "From roaming about on the earth and walking around on it." The LORD said to **Satan**, "Have you considered My servant Job? For there is no one like him on the earth, a blameless and upright man, fearing God and turning away from*

*evil." Then **Satan** answered the LORD, "Does Job fear God for nothing? "Have You not made a hedge about him and his house and all that he has, on every side? You have blessed the work of his hands, and his possessions have increased in the land. "But put forth Your hand now and touch all that he has; he will surely curse You to Your face." Then the LORD said to **Satan**, "Behold, all that he has is in your power, only do not put forth your hand on him." So **Satan** departed from the presence of the LORD. Now on the day when his sons and his daughters were eating and drinking wine in their oldest brother's house, a messenger came to Job and said, "The oxen were plowing and the donkeys feeding beside them, and the Sabeans attacked and took them. They also slew the servants with the edge of the sword, and I alone have escaped to tell you." While he was still speaking, another also came and said, "The fire of God fell from heaven and burned up the sheep and the servants and consumed them, and I alone have escaped to tell you." While he was still speaking, another also came and said, "The Chaldeans formed three bands and made a raid on the camels and took them and slew the servants with the edge of the sword, and I alone have escaped to tell you." While he was still speaking, another also came and said, "Your sons and your daughters were eating and drinking wine in their oldest brother's house, and behold, a great wind came from across the wilderness and struck the four corners of the house, and it fell on the young people and they died, and I alone have escaped to tell you." Then Job arose and tore his robe and shaved his head,*

*and he fell to the ground and worshiped. He said,
"Naked I came from my mother's womb, And
naked I shall return there. The LORD gave and
the LORD has taken away. Blessed be the name of
the LORD." Through all this Job did not sin nor
did he blame God.*

How did Lucifer oppose Job? He destroyed everything
Job cared about. He openly opposed his life. Lucifer used his
businesses, his family, his houses, and his friends as a part of
his oppositional scheme against Job. And yet it did not work!
It actually drove Job closer to God, not further away from
him.

Sometimes Satan only opposes us in one area of life, like
our finances or our marriage. This can be very frustrating but
if we are able to resist Satan's resistance and continue to push
forward with the righteousness we have been called to
accomplish, we end up closer to God and stronger than
before.

Exercises to Defeat Satan

How do we defeat Satan as he and his demons oppose us
and send enemies against us? There are eight actions and
spiritual antidotes that are known as the Armor of God that
are essential to winning the life God has always wanted for
you. They will be a crucial part of beating the opposition of
Satan. Satan wants to destroy us and add us to his manure
pile of wasted people, wasted skills, wasted opportunities, and
wasted lives. But we can win the life that God has planned for
us through Christ. God has given us all we need; we just have
to start using all that he has provided.

These spiritual weapons are truth, righteousness, peace, faith, salvation, Word of God (God's Wisdom), prayer, and alertness. The Devil acts against these qualities because in order to destroy a life, he needs to distort or attack each of these. In every scheme there is an attack against, or distortion of, one of these spiritual realities. It is these qualities that bring health, blessing, peace, and joy to people.

Let me write these again in a graphically interesting way so you will hopefully remember them. Memorize them. Use them. Write your own copy of them. Draw them. Embroider them. Ask God for insight on how to increase their use in your life. You and I will need these to defeat the Schemes of the Satan.

Truth

Righteousness

Peace

Faith

Salvation

Word of God

Prayer

Alertness

With these we have the answers, the antidotes, and the super-weapons that will defeat Satan's opposition. We also have the Holy Spirit guiding us as to which one to use at what time. Each of these spiritual weapons is a scheme buster, but we are to be guided by the Holy Spirit in our deployment of these weapons. We don't just use all the weapons every time we sense a spiritual attack; there are usually one or two that need our focus at a time. There are numerous examples in Scripture where the Holy Spirit directed people to use only one or two weapons instead of all of them (Matt. 4:1-12; Matt. 26:36-46). When I am under attack, I pray down through these spiritual weapons and ask God to guide me to just the right one for the particular temptation I am facing.

Now it is important to note that the first three spiritual weapons are to be deployed constantly in your life. As the Apostle Paul outlines, these spiritual weapons are distinct between the first three and the last five.

> *Stand firm therefore, <u>HAVING</u> GIRDED YOUR LOINS WITH TRUTH, and <u>HAVING</u> PUT ON THE BREASTPLATE OF RIGHTEOUSNESS, and <u>having</u> shod YOUR FEET WITH THE PREPARATION OF THE GOSPEL OF PEACE; in addition to all, taking up the shield of faith with which you will be able to extinguish all the flaming arrows of the evil one. And take THE HELMET OF SALVATION, and the sword of the Spirit, which is the word of God. With all prayer and petition pray at all times in the Spirit, and with this in view, be on the alert with all perseverance and petition for all the saints. (Eph. 6:14-18)*

Notice that for the first three, he uses the past tense verb *of having*, as in already in the past having put on these weapons: Truth, Righteousness, and Peace. You are always to be standing on truth and learning more. We are always to be righteous and loving. We are always to be peaceable and forgiving. The last five weapons are to be taken up and deployed when the battle rages: Faith, Salvation, Word of God, Prayer, and Alertness.

Engaging God in Your Spiritual Battle with Satan

Just as Jesus was completely dependent upon the Father and the Spirit, we are dependent upon the whole of the Trinity for our victory in the spiritual battles of our life. Too many Christians act like they are on their own when facing Satan. They think God threw the manual (Bible) at them and told them, "Read it; all the answers are in there." God is with us and has prepared all the weapons, knows the right strategy, and will give us wisdom and guidance if we ask for it and expect to receive it. Seriously ask God in prayer the following questions when you think Satan is opposing you.

What spiritual weapon should I to use against **Satan's internal opposition and external enemies?**

- Is it truth?
- Is it righteousness?
- Is it peace?
- Is it faith or God-ordained risk?
- Is it a God-provided way of escape or element of hope?
- Is it wisdom from God's Word?
- Is it prayer?
- Is it alertness and precaution?

Once you have answered these questions, then it is time to go deeper on the particular weapons you are supposed to deploy. In the exercises that follow I have made a lot of educated guesses about what you may need to defeat a particular scheme, but it is more important that you stay sensitive to the Lord Jesus as he guides you to the particular way of using the Armor of God to defeat the schemes of Satan. It is also very helpful to have a pastor, mentor, life coach, wise friend, or counselor help you understand how to defeat the enemy. When you are facing repeated opposition to good works and righteous ideas, internally ask these questions and act to protect yourself. Satan's opposition and enemies are tests of our resolve. God loves us and wants us to get through this test and be stronger on the other side. If you are going after some good thing, plan, or some righteous development, then you can expect to have opposition and enemies. Satan is always trying to block us from the abundant life God has planned. Don't fall for it.

Further Questions to Ask

Pray down through these questions and let God the Holy Spirit guide you to the particular spiritual weapon that he wants you to deploy against Satan's internal opposition and/or external enemies.

What **truth(s)** would stop **Satan's internal opposition and/or external enemies** and deliver the individual, group, or nation?

- It may be truths about God that will win the day.
- It may be truths about Christian living that will win the day.
- It may be truths about ourselves that will win the day.
- It may be truths about others and/or society that will win the day.
- It may be a particular scientific fact or historical field that will dispel the deception and schemes of the enemy.

What **righteousness, love, or morality** would stop **Satan's internal opposition and/or external enemies** and deliver the individual, group, or nation?

- It may be that you need to increase your love in one of the relationships of your life.
- It may be that you need to increase the wisdom of the love in one of your relationships.
- It may be that you need to do good and right things that you have not been doing.
- It may be that you need to stop doing some unloving, unrighteous, or damaging actions or words.
- It may be that you need to ask about an opportunity you are being given:
  - Will this actually do good? Will this harm others?
  - Is this really just about my desire and I am being led along by my desire?

What **peace moves** or strategies would stop **Satan's internal opposition and/or external enemies** and deliver the individual, group, or nation?

- It may be that you need to make peace with God in ways that you haven't yet.
- It may be that you need to examine or lower your expectations or the anger will still win.
- It may be that you need to change some of your actions or the circumstances that surround the tense moments in your life.
- It may be that you need to forgive God, yourself, or others to defeat this scheme.
- It may be that you need to turn this enemy into a friend.

- It may be that you need to stop acting with hostility in a particular situation.
- It may be that you need to start positive steps to bring about peace with others.
- It may be that you need to leave all justice with God.
- It may be that you need more than just peace; you need harmony with another person.

What **faith steps** or God-directed risks would stop **Satan's internal opposition and/or external enemies** and deliver the individual, group, or nation?

- It may be that you need to trust God for something that is right but very hard to do.
- It may be that you need to learn more about God and the Christian life so that your trust is more solid and informed.
- It may be that God wants you to trust him and head in a new direction to defeat this particular scheme of the Devil.
- It may be that you need to decide to trust God when it doesn't feel like the best solution.
- It may be that you must trust God when you are making no progress as that is better than the progress toward the wrong goals.

What **ways of escape (salvation) or hope** would stop **Satan's internal opposition and/or external enemies** and deliver the individual, group, or nation?

- It may be that you need to explore and take fuller advantage of the salvation that is in the Lord Jesus Christ than you have in the past.
- It may be that you are supposed to take some way of escape that will get you out of a situation that is too tempting, too pressurized, too dangerous, or too life altering for you.
- It may be that you must hold on to or look for the elements of hope from your past and in the present as you wait for God's deliverance.
- It may be that you have to cling to the hope of your salvation: the return of Christ and your place in heaven to say *no* to the temptations of the Devil in this life.

What **wisdom from God's Word** would stop **Satan's internal opposition and/or external enemies** and deliver the individual, group, or nation?

- It may be that you need to read the Scriptures daily so that God can prompt you with the appropriate verses when you need them.
- It may be that you need to read through the Scriptures so that you have a grasp of what God is saying in the whole of the Word of God.
- It may be that you need to go to a class, seminar, or small group where you can get a better overview of the Old and New Testament.
- It may be that you need to learn how to study the Scriptures so that when God prompts you with a verse, you can study it and gain the appropriate understanding of what God is saying.

- It may be that you need to learn how to meditate on the Word of God so that when God gives you a Scripture, you know how to carry it around in your mind all day.
- It may be that you need to quote a verse of Scripture to yourself all day to defeat the scheme the Devil is running.
- It may be that you need to quote a particular verse of Scripture at the Devil to let him know that you are on to his scheme. You now know the wisdom of God and will not be fooled by his ideas and opportunities.

What **kind and type of prayers** would stop **Satan's internal opposition and/or external enemies** and deliver the individual, group, or nation?

- It may be that God prompts you to spend time praising him as the antidote to a particular scheme of the Devil.
- It may be that God wants you to prayerfully contemplate a Scripture as the way to win against a particular scheme.
- It may be that God wants you to request certain things from him that you will need to win against this particular scheme.
- It may be that God wants you to pray for someone else to defeat this scheme.
- It may be that you need to pray prayers of gratefulness in order to pass the test that is being thrown at you.
- It may be that you need to confess your sins or the sins of the group or your nation in order to stop this scheme from succeeding.
- It may be that God wants you to battle for the unconverted soul(s) you know that need the Lord in order to defeat this particular scheme of the Devil.

- It may be that you need to pray for government officials that they would be safe and ethical as they make decisions, unthreatened by interests groups that are evil.

What **precautions and/or alertness** would stop **Satan's internal opposition and/or external enemies** and deliver the individual, group, or nation?

- It may be that God wants you to make very specific preparations to withstand a scheme or test of the Devil.
- It may be that you have an exposed weakness to sin that will damage, dishonor, or destroy you if it is not dealt with; and you must protect yourself and your loved ones in some way before the storm of the test arrives.

- It may be that you do not know enough about a crucial relationship or truth of Christianity, and God is giving you the heads-up about learning how to make that right. You must act before the test comes, or it will hurt you or stop your progress.

Scheme #4

The Roaring Lion Scheme
(Amplified Fear)

One of the most interesting exercises I have given to my students is to have them tell me their first memories of money. When did money become "money" to you? What emotions were connected to money for you? In almost every case one of the dominant emotions is fear. One person, who was completely controlled by a fear from their childhood, talked about how they grew up poor and embraced the fear of not having enough to eat at a very early age. He vowed to never be like that again, so he worked multiple jobs and drove himself to ridiculous extremes to heap up piles of money to avoid feeling the fear of not having enough to eat ever again. Unfortunately in a number of cases his fears drove him to live an unbalanced life so there was never any time to spend with family and friends. There was always more money to be made and fear to be pushed back. Another person exploring the power of money remembers being told that his family did not have the money to buy the nice new bicycle like the other kids so that young man felt inferior for the hand-me-down bike he was riding. When his parents saved and purchased the new bike like all the other kids, it was quickly stolen and the fear-based impression was made that said, "You are not worthy and even if you get nice things they will be taken from you." It became a mantra that controlled this man's life for years until he discovered it was sourced in a spirit of fear.

Fear is such a powerful emotion. It is normal and can be healthy; but it also can be debilitating, controlling, and paralyzing. It can also be a scheme of the Devil. The Scriptures tell us that *fear* is one of the major schemes of the Devil by referring to him as a roaring lion and a dragon. Both of these animals were designed to produce fear at various levels. This *Roaring Lion Scheme* we will now talk about is one of the Devil's favorite weapons to control and stop people. In every major relationship there is the potential of being bullied by our fears. Our fears can act as a gatekeeper, stopping us from the really good thing we could be doing.

In many cases our fears are not ours at all; they are spiritual attacks sourced in a spirit of fear and we have chosen to own it, giving it power to control our thoughts, speech, and actions. I have worked with many people who were almost completely controlled by their fears—about money, about their marriage, about their career and/or employment. Whatever the fear, we must face it, find out its source, and push past it to the great life that resides on the other side of our fears. If we don't face our fears, we will live in a prison of our own making, shut up into a much smaller life than God intended. Many times a person's life is bordered on each side by a fear that the person has never pushed through. In every case where fear is the boundary, it means that there is something better just beyond our fears; we just have to push through to grasp it. Jesus says, "I came that you might have life and have it abundantly." A fear-based life is not the abundant life.

I can remember one woman who allowed fear to almost destroy her marriage and family. It was a spiritual attack, but it took us a while to figure it out. She insisted that her marriage was on the rocks even though neither of them could point to a legitimate reason. She was moving away from her marriage even though she said that she wanted it to make it. After a number of sessions I focused on fear as the driving feeling for the struggles in her marriage. As a young girl she experienced her parents' divorce when she was thirteen years of age. This event so scared her that she embraced the fear that it would happen to her. When her oldest child was nearing her thirteenth birthday, she began acting in a cold and distant way to her husband. Her whole demeanor changed towards him. Both husband and wife told me that they loved each other, and they did not know what this change was all about. When I made the connection to her parents' divorce, the emotions came pouring out. She had become convinced that when her daughter turned thirteen her husband would come home one night and announce that he was having an affair and leave the family just like her father had done with her mother and their family so many years before. It took several months of listening, teaching, and praying for her to confront this spirit of fear that had settled on her.

This scheme is really all about fear at its various levels. God calls the Devil the *Roaring Lion* and the *Dragon* to help us understand this strategy he employs that uses levels of fear to keep us from the life we were meant to have. In our modern day we would call these levels *anxiety, fear, and terror*. These represent various kinds of emotional attacks that have a spiritual element to them. Let me be clear; not all fear is from the Devil but some is. It is this spiritual-sourced fear that this chapter will help you uncover and push through.

The Roaring Lion—Use of Fear, Panic, and Anxiety Attacks

Be of sober spirit, be on the alert. Your adversary, the Devil, prowls around like a roaring lion, seeking someone to devour. *(1 Peter 5:8)*

In the wild, the roaring lion herds his prey through anxiety and fear into the mouth of the lionesses that do the hunting. The roaring lion is trying to get panic-induced movement away from the roar. That is usually the exact wrong direction to move. The roaring lion is challenging but largely harmless. It is the quiet, aggressive lions that need to be watched. The roaring lion is trying to produce anxiety, fear, and terror without fighting. His roar is often a part of a ploy to get the animal to run into a trap. Really, the proper direction the animal should run is almost always toward the sound of the roar. The older, slower lions do the roaring; and the quiet, strong lionesses do the hunting of the prey driven to them by the roaring.

Likewise, the Devil as the Roaring Lion uses anxiety, fear, and terror to drive people into traps that will destroy or control their lives. Often when fear is roaring at you, the way of escape is to go right towards the fear just like antelope would be smart to run towards the sound of the roar because the least amount of harm is that way.

Fear often begins with a normal uncertainty, but it can grow into an overwhelming phobia if it is not understood and resisted appropriately. The Devil uses *The Roaring Lion Scheme* by amplifying fear, anxiety, and/or terror to make a run at you with various levels of your fears. At times these fears can be overwhelming. Internally, he may send the fears in your dreams or into your thoughts. Externally, he could send a real version of your fears at you in real life. He wants you to stop doing something you are doing or to not take the steps you are about to take.

I have run across a number of people who have suffered from panic and anxiety attacks. Sometimes these have had a spiritual source and many times it is an emotional or psychological issue that needs to be worked through. If the anxiety or panic attack responds to prayer in its various forms (biblical meditation, confession, and/or worship), then it has a spiritual component. If these spiritual exercises have no affect on the panic or anxiety attack, then the attack is sourced somewhere else other than the spiritual world.

I can remember working with a man we will call George, who was going through struggles at work. In the midst of the uncertainty he was attacked with a level of fear he had never known before. George was vulnerable in his life because he put his trust in a paycheck and an employer rather than God. This gave the Devil the opening to run *The Roaring Lion Scheme* on him. He reported that the fear of losing his job was everywhere and left him paralyzed. This is what the Roaring Lion does: he amplifies normal anxieties into a full mental picture of our greatest fears. If George gave in and began acting out of his fear instead of moving wisely through the crisis of life, he would have made impulsive decisions, self-focused choices, and limited his future possibilities.

I was working with one couple where the husband was suddenly overwhelmed with anxiety. This was new for him and he was quite dumbfounded. His prayers and spiritual work made little dent in the problem; but when his wife prayed for him, the anxiety stopped immediately. This type of phenomena usually means that one of the triggering components is a family problem that cannot be addressed by just one person's prayers. The whole family must engage spiritually on the presenting problem and the spiritual attack.

It's important to consider spiritual elements as the source of a panic or anxiety attack so you can deal with it appropriately.

Amplified Fear – The Use of Terror, Extreme Fear

We get our ideas of terror most commonly through war and terrorism. Terror is frightening at the highest levels because there seems to be no sure motive for why it strikes, who brings it, or when it will strike. Terror produces fear at the highest levels because it strikes without warning; it seems random. The Devil is involved in prompting terror and using it to paralyze people from doing the good they are supposed to do. The biblical image of terror is of a Dragon—a mythical beast that can unleash immense destruction with no personal motive -- just its own wanton appetite. The Bible gives the Devil the title Dragon when he is unleashing terror, violence, and destructive power as he will in the last days before Christ returns. We will return to this idea when we explore the Dragon Scheme more closely but understand that fear, terror, and anxiety are a part of the arsenal of the Devil.

Satan uses terror to destroy the good, and the above means are simply ways for him to terrorize. Satan will use fear to prod, move, control, and stop people. But Satan uses this amplified fear technique when he uses the most extreme form of fear to paralyze people from making any form of progress toward righteousness. Terror is the highest form of fear because of its randomness. There is no way of knowing where it is coming from, when it is coming, and through whom it is coming.

Over the years of my counseling and spiritual guidance of thousands of people, I have had people relate grueling periods of terror in their lives that needed to be processed so they could get back to the full potential that God had for their lives. Their lives bear scars, but they can live an abundant life in Christ in spite of the terror of a previous part of their life. Let me help you understand a quick overview of some of the ways that the Devil becomes the Dragon by unleashing terror in people's lives.

Childhood—being raped or molested by a relative or friend of the family; being sold for sex by your mother or father; being physically beaten for random infractions; never knowing when your parents would come home drunk and what they would do when it happened; your parents' inconsistent employment which necessitates constant moving; your parents' involvement in illegal activities which means hiding from the authorities.

These and many other things can terrorize children and cause them to give up on their dreams. They never know when the terror will strike. They can't think about the future, only about the present and how to avoid the terror the next time it comes if they can. The Devil uses all that is involved in terror to destroy lives. He wants people to give in to the terror and abandon plans for good, hope for the future, and ethical behavior.

Teenage years—having the increasing possibility of having a shooting at your school or in your neighborhood; your parents' divorce; being physically or relationally bullied at school or in the neighborhood; being cyber stalked and/or cyber bullied; having your boyfriend or girlfriend dump you or shame you in some way to your peer group.

These are terror moments for teens but also include all the other terror issues that were mentioned above under childhood terror. Terror makes you give up because there is no rhyme or reason to the destruction. You can't discern a pattern or a way to get out of its way; that is what is terrifying. The Devil is right now terrorizing some teenagers in these ways and pushing them to abandon their dreams for a great life that would make a difference for everyone around them. They need to be aware of how to resist Satan and hang on to their dreams.

Adulthood—having your identity stolen; losing a job suddenly or randomly; being called into active service in a war; being caught up in a terrorist attack; being at a bank, store, or public place in the midst of a robbery or hostage situation; being forced to pay for protection from some shady characters because the authorities won't protect you or your family; a natural disaster wiping out your home or place of employment.

Again, let me say that the Devil has a hand in all of these terror issues even though he usually convinces some person or organization to actually do the terrorizing. The idea is to get you to abandon your dreams, goals, and good works and accept the present moment and present relative safety as the most you can hope for.

It's difficult to make yourself safe from terror, so it is even more paralyzing. The Devil can destabilize a country through corruption and war. He can destabilize a family through inconsistent employment or poverty. Everyone gives up on the good they want to do and takes a selfish view bent on just surviving. If we cannot discover a reason for our fear, then it haunts us in ways that are the most disturbing. When something terrible happens to you and yet it is random or unexpected, then it is likely *The Fear Scheme* is being used against you so you'll give up on the large goals and dreams of your life.

Internal and External Versions

We know there are at least three levels to this fear scheme: anxiety, fear, and terror. But there are also internal and external versions of this fear scheme. If the attack is an internal scheme, then a small fear may be magnified until it is overwhelming. Fear is not always a scheme of the Devil, but it is when anxiety, fear, or terror is amplified to the place where good stops, dreams cease, and when goals are abandoned. This is how you know *The Roaring Lion Scheme* is being used. It is almost like a spirit of fear descends on you and hyper alerts you to every danger or concern or magnifies a particular one out of proportion.

An external version of *The Roaring Lion Scheme* may come through a person whose own actions induce anxiety, fear, or terror in you. It could be that your spouse's spending habits begin to bring anxiety. It could be that your children's choice of friends begins to make you afraid. It could be that a boss or colleague begins acting in a new way toward you that makes you nervous, anxious, or afraid. They are responding to the Devil's prompting and becoming an unwitting tool to produce fear in you. It could be that a mentally unstable person made threats or shot people in a mall near you. It could be that a thief has been breaking into houses in your neighborhood or broke into your house and stole a number of prized possessions. It could be that one of the above possibilities of childhood, teenage, and/or adult terror invaded your life. Do not give in to fear. Yes, you are afraid and it will make you more cautious; but it should not force you to give up your dreams, goals, and relationships. Fear is a test to see how much you want to do something that is good.

The way you pass the test is by persevering and continuing to move forward.

Exercises to Defeat The Roaring Lion

How do we defeat the Devil as he uses fear, anxiety, or terror on us? There are eight actions and spiritual antidotes known as the Armor of God that are essential to winning the life God has always wanted for you. They will be a crucial part of beating the temptations of the Devil. The Devil wants to destroy us and add us to his manure pile of wasted people, wasted skills, wasted opportunities, and wasted lives. But we can win the life that God has planned for us through Christ. God has given us all we need; we just have to start using all that he has provided.

These spiritual weapons are truth, righteousness, peace, faith, salvation, Word of God (God's Wisdom), prayer, and alertness. The Devil acts against these qualities because in order to destroy a life, he needs to distort or attack each of these. In every scheme there is an attack against, or distortion of, one of these spiritual realities. It is these qualities that bring health, blessing, peace, and joy to people.

Let me write these again in a graphically interesting way so you will hopefully remember them. Memorize them. Use them. Write your own copy of them. Draw them. Ask God for insight on how to increase their use in your life. You and I will need these to defeat the Schemes of the Devil.

Truth

Righteousness

Peace

Faith

Salvation

Word of God

Prayer

Alertness

With these weapons, we have the answers, the antidotes, and the super-weapons that will defeat the Devil's use of fear to paralyze us. We also have the Holy Spirit guiding us as to which one to use at what time. Each of these spiritual weapons is a scheme buster, but we are to be guided by the Holy Spirit in our deployment of these weapons. We don't just use all the weapons every time we sense a spiritual attack; there are usually one or two that need our focus at a time. There are numerous examples in Scripture where the Holy Spirit directed people to use only one or two weapons instead of all of them (Matt. 4:1-12; Matt. 26:36-46). When I am under attack, I pray down through these spiritual weapons and ask God to guide me to just the right one for the fear, anxiety, or terror I am facing.

Now it is important to note that the first three spiritual weapons are to be deployed constantly in your life. As the Apostle Paul outlines, these spiritual weapons are distinct between the first three and the last five.

Stand firm therefore, <u>HAVING</u> GIRDED YOUR LOINS WITH TRUTH, and <u>HAVING</u> PUT ON THE BREASTPLATE OF RIGHTEOUSNESS, and <u>having</u> shod YOUR FEET WITH THE PREPARATION OF THE GOSPEL OF PEACE; in addition to all, taking up the shield of faith with which you will be able to extinguish all *the flaming arrows of the evil one. And take THE HELMET OF SALVATION, and the sword of the Spirit, which is the word of God. With all prayer and petition pray at all times in the Spirit, and with this in view, be on the alert with all perseverance and petition for all the saints, (Eph. 6:14-18).*

Notice that for the first three, he uses the past tense verb *of having,* as in already in the past having put on these weapons: Truth, Righteousness, and Peace. You are always to be standing on truth and learning more. We are always to be righteous and loving. We are always to be peaceable and forgiving. The last five weapons are to be taken up and deployed when the battle rages: Faith, Salvation, Word of God, Prayer, and Alertness.

Engaging God in Your Spiritual Battle with the Roaring Lion

Just as Jesus was completely dependent upon the Father and the Spirit, we are dependent upon the whole of the Trinity for our victory in the spiritual battles of our life. Too many Christians act like they are on their own when facing the Devil. They think God threw the manual (Bible) at them and told them, "Read it; all the answers are in there." God is with us and has prepared all the weapons, knows the right strategy, and will give us wisdom and guidance if we ask for it and expect to receive it. Seriously ask God the following questions when you think the Devil is tempting, testing, or scheming against you.

What spiritual weapon should I to use against **fear, anxiety, and/or terror?**

- Is it truth?
- Is it righteousness?
- Is it peace?
- Is it faith or God-ordained risk?
- Is it a God-provided way of escape or element of hope?
- Is it wisdom from God's Word?
- Is it prayer?
- Is it alertness and precaution?

Once you have answered these questions, then it is time to go deeper on the particular weapons you are supposed to deploy. In the exercises that follow I have made a lot of educated guesses about what you may need to defeat a particular scheme, but it is more important that you stay sensitive to the Lord Jesus as he guides you to the particular way of using the Armor of God to defeat the schemes of Satan. It is also very helpful to have a pastor, mentor, life coach, wise friend, or counselor help you understand how to defeat the enemy. When you are facing repeated fears, anxiety, and terror from others, internally ask these questions and act to protect yourself. The Devil's fears, anxiety, and terror are not real. God loves us and wants us to get through this test and be stronger on the other side. If it sounds too good to be true, it probably is. If everybody else is saying that this group or theory is wrong, then it has a chance of being wrong. The Devil is always leading away from the abundant life God has planned. Don't fall for it.

Further Questions to Ask

Pray down through these questions and let God the Holy Spirit guide you to the particular spiritual weapon that he wants you to deploy against the fears, anxiety, and terror you are facing.

What **truth(s)** would stop these **fears, anxieties, and/or terrors** and deliver the individual, group, or nation?

- It may be truths about God that will win the day.
- It may be truths about Christian living that will win the day.
- It may be truths about ourselves that will win the day.
- It may be truths about others and/or society that will win the day.
- It may be a particular scientific fact or historical field that will dispel the deception and schemes of the enemy.

What **righteousness, love, or morality** would stop these **fears, anxieties, and/or terrors** and deliver the individual, group, or nation?

- It may be that you need to increase your love in one of the relationships of your life.
- It may be that you need to increase the wisdom of the love in one of your relationships.
- It may be that you need to do good and right things that you have not been doing.
- It may be that you need to stop doing some unloving, unrighteous, or damaging actions or words.

- It may be that you need to ask about an opportunity you are being given:
  - Will this actually do good? Will this harm others?
  - Is this really just about my desire and I am being led along by my desire?

What **peace moves** or strategies would stop these **fears, anxieties, and/or terrors** and deliver the individual, group, or nation?

- It may be that you need to make peace with God in ways that you haven't yet.
- It may be that you need to examine or lower your expectations or the anger will still win.
- It may be that you need to change some of your actions or the circumstances that surround the tense moments in your life.
- It may be that you need to forgive God, yourself, or others to defeat this scheme.
- It may be that you need to turn this enemy into a friend.
- It may be that you need to stop acting with hostility in a particular situation.
- It may be that you need to start positive steps to bring about peace with others.
- It may be that you need to leave all justice with God.
- It may be that you need more than just peace; you need harmony with another person.

What **faith steps** or God-directed risks would stop these **fears, anxieties, and/or terrors** and deliver the individual, group, or nation?

- It may be that you need to trust God for something that is right but very hard to do.
- It may be that you need to learn more about God and the Christian life so that your trust is more solid and informed.
- It may be that God wants you to trust him and head in a new direction to defeat this particular scheme of the Devil.
- It may be that you need to decide to trust God when it doesn't feel like the best solution.
- It may be that you must trust God when you are making no progress as that is better than the progress toward the wrong goals.

What **ways of escape (salvation) or hope** would stop these **fears, anxieties, and/or terrors** and deliver the individual, group, or nation?

- It may be that you need to explore and take fuller advantage of the salvation that is in the Lord Jesus Christ than you have in the past.
- It may be that you are supposed to take some way of escape that will get you out of a situation that is too tempting, too pressurized, too dangerous, or too life altering for you.
- It may be that you must hold on to or look for the elements of hope from your past and in the present as you wait for God's deliverance.

- It may be that you have to cling to the hope of your salvation: the return of Christ and your place in heaven to say *no* to the temptations of the Devil in this life.

What **wisdom from God's Word** would stop these **fears, anxieties, and/or terrors** and deliver the individual, group, or nation?

- It may be that you need to read the Scriptures daily so that God can prompt you with the appropriate verses when you need them.
- It may be that you need to read through the Scriptures so that you have a grasp of what God is saying in the whole of the Word of God.
- It may be that you need to go to a class, seminar, or small group where you can get a better overview of the Old and New Testament.
- It may be that you need to learn how to study the Scriptures so that when God prompts you with a verse, you can study it and gain the appropriate understanding of what God is saying.
- It may be that you need to learn how to meditate on the Word of God so that when God gives you a Scripture, you know how to carry it around in your mind all day.
- It may be that you need to quote a verse of Scripture to yourself all day to defeat the scheme the Devil is running.
- It may be that you need to quote a particular verse of Scripture at the Devil to let him know that you are on to his scheme. You now know the wisdom of God and will not be fooled by his ideas and opportunities.

What **kind and type of prayers** would stop these **fears, anxieties, and/or terrors** and deliver the individual, group, or nation?

- It may be that God prompts you to spend time praising him as the antidote to a particular scheme of the Devil.
- It may be that God wants you to prayerfully contemplate a Scripture as the way to win against a particular scheme.
- It may be that God wants you to request certain things from him that you will need to win against this particular scheme.
- It may be that God wants you to pray for someone else to defeat this scheme.
- It may be that you need to pray prayers of gratefulness in order to pass the test that is being thrown at you.
- It may be that you need to confess your sins or the sins of the group or your nation in order to stop this scheme from succeeding.
- It may be that God wants you to battle for the unconverted soul(s) you know that need the Lord in order to defeat this particular scheme of the Devil.
- It may be that you need to pray for government officials that they would be safe and ethical as they make decisions unthreatened by interests groups that are evil.

What **precautions and/or alertness** would stop these **fears, anxieties, and/or terrors** and deliver the individual, group, or nation?

- It may be that God wants you to make very specific preparations to withstand a scheme or test of the Devil.

- It may be that you have an exposed weakness to sin that will damage, dishonor, or destroy you if it is not dealt with; and you must protect yourself and your loved ones in some way before the storm of the test arrives.

- It may be that you do not know enough about a crucial relationship or truth of Christianity and God is giving you the heads-up about learning how to make that right. You must act before the test comes, or it will hurt you or stop your progress.

Schemes #5

The Angel of Light Scheme
(Amplified Spiritual Power and Wisdom)

A young woman we will call Nancy began coming to the church where I pastored. After about a year, Nancy approached me after a service.

She said, "Pastor, I think I have a problem."

I replied, "What kind of problem?"

She said, "My son sleeps above his bed."

I, of course, was dumbfounded and asked for clarification. She went on to explain this strange phenomenon that had been happening nearly every night for a while. When she put her son to sleep at night, she tucked him under the covers. Later in the night she would check on him, and he would be hovering above the bed. Obviously this was strange, so I dug deeper about the situation. After much discussion and prayer, she told me that before she came to our church and our town, her boy had become sick and was oozing puss out of his eyes. She did not trust the doctors, so she went to a shaman who prayed over the boy and put an ointment on his eyes. After that incident, the young boy began to hover above his bed in the middle of the night. He had been healed from his eye problem but was clearly being disturbed in the spiritual realm. The Devil had run *The Spiritual Power Scheme* on the family and they had fallen for it. They had been awed by the spiritual power that the shaman wielded. They wanted their boy healed no matter how it happened. What they didn't know was that the shaman tapped into a power that was satanic in origin.

We walked the mother through prayers of confession and renunciation of any place or power she and her husband had given to Satan by visiting this shaman and allowing him to do his magic over the boy. They claimed their place as spiritual authorities over their boy and cut off the agreement that they had given to the Devil. After that the boy no longer hovered over his bed, and later the husband even gave his life to Christ. The whole family followed Christ from then on and together they learned to live as Christians. She had fallen victim to *The Angel of Light Scheme* of Satan, but they all were eventually delivered.

In the story I just told, we see a prime example of another scheme of Satan which is getting lots of attention in these days—*The Angel of Light Scheme.* Today we see lots of people who want to be spiritual and have spiritual experiences without Jesus Christ, without a church, and without any thought that there may be both good and bad spiritual powers. This quest for spiritual experiences can be used by the Devil to run a spiritual power and wisdom scheme where he and his demons show themselves to people, demonstrating their ability to perform false miracles and offering supernatural "wisdom" in order to convince people that the false is true. This is nothing new; it can be seen throughout Scripture and throughout church history over thousands of years.

In this chapter I will give you Scriptural and personal examples of how this Angel of Light scheme is being used on people. This next story is a true story that comes out of my files from working with people who have fallen for various schemes of Satan. They are examples of how they became caught up in seeking spiritual experiences.

The Prince of the Power of the Air

In Ephesians 2:1-3, the Apostle Paul refers to the Devil as the Prince of the Power of the Air. This title suggests invisible power that moves through the air without being seen. It is spiritual power that is beyond our physical and visible realm.

> *And you were dead in your trespasses and sins, in which you formerly walked according to the course of this world, according to **the prince of the power of the air**, of the spirit that is now working in the sons of disobedience. Among them we too all formerly lived in the lusts of our flesh, indulging the desires of the flesh and of the mind, and were by nature children of wrath, even as the rest. (Eph. 2:1-3)*

The Apostle is telling us that the Devil has the ability to use demonic power -- an invisible power used to control people and events over great distances. I can remember working with one man who faithfully tried to pray for his wife. His wife, however, was unwilling to repent from the demonic attachments that had her bound. Whenever the man prayed for her that she would be free from the oppression and control that gripped her, he would experience a choking sensation and would often be overwhelmed with anxiety and depression. We eventually needed to have him stop praying for his wife until he was stronger in his faith and she had repented of some of the occultic sins she had committed. She eventually realized what was happening in and through her and changed her mind about the things that had happened to her and the things that she had done. She no longer gave a place for the enemy to operate in her life. She was free, and her husband was freed up to pray for his wife and family.

Another young man I had the privilege of working with became a Christian before I met him. He was making great progress in loving the Lord Jesus and the Bible. He was growing and changing right before everyone's eyes. Before he had become a Christian, he had been rude and self-absorbed; but under the guiding hand of the Lord Jesus Christ, he became loving and kind. But because of a lack of spiritual discernment, he opened himself to *The Angel of Light Scheme* of Satan. After a year of being a Christian and having experienced a complete turnaround in his life, he met some Christians who told him that he needed to learn to speak in tongues in order to move to the next level of being a Christian. He studied with these folks and became convinced to pray, asking God to give him the gift of speaking in other tongues. He finally received the gift and began to practice this prayer language regularly. After a while of this he noticed that the more he practiced the prayer language, the less he felt like reading his Bible. He became more and more absorbed in the gift and less in reading the Bible and getting together with other Christians. One night while praying in tongues, he blacked out. When he came to, he was on all fours on the floor, playing with himself sexually. He realized that something was definitely wrong, and he contacted me after this bizarre, spiritual episode. Together we were able to uncover that his overwhelming desire for more spiritual experiences had opened him up to a counterfeit gift of tongues. He had fallen for *The Angel of Light Scheme.* He was so excited about the power of Christ in his life that he wanted more spiritual power. Unfortunately he did not distinguish *the source* of the spiritual power. After he renounced the counterfeit gift of tongues and returned his focus to the Lord Jesus Christ and the Scriptures, the gentle guiding of the Holy Spirit returned and his righteous, growing spiritual life returned.

The Angel of Light

In 2 Corinthians 11:13-14, the Apostle Paul refers to the Devil as an Angel of Light.

> *For such men are false apostles, deceitful workers, disguising themselves as apostles of Christ. No wonder, for even Satan disguises himself as an* **angel of light.**

In this passage the Apostle Paul warned the Corinthian believers that just as there are false apostles, there are false angels; and Satan himself disguises himself as an *Angel of Light*. This is a Greek phrase *"angelos phos,"* which means a spiritual messenger of great light. The Devil uses this spiritual light as a deceptive tool that causes people to listen to what he is saying and selling. It is all a part of the sting. Using spiritual realities and spiritual power to deceive and derail, the Devil or his demons will appear to a person as an angel or as a being outside of the normal physical universe and reveal information that is beyond our knowledge. Their hope is to bring the person along into their employ, following their orders and eventually falling into sin at the behest of the angelic or extraterrestrial being. There is great danger and great oppression if one falls for this satanic scheme.

Here is another example of the Devil disguising himself as an angel of light in one woman's life. One woman came to see me for spiritual counseling. She shared a story with me about how at one point in her life she wanted to experience spiritual power. She went to a revivalist meeting where there were significant demonstrations of spiritual power. She came forward and asked for this spiritual power to be revealed to her. She was so excited and she didn't think about the actual source of the spiritual power. Soon an angel appeared to her. She said it was wonderful. This angel kept visiting her and giving her messages. This was what she was looking for. She had wanted spiritual experiences, and she was having them in a huge way. Later she came to visit me because something did not seem right even though she experienced significant spiritual events and angels continued to appear to her. She was told that she would be a prophetess for this heavenly messenger. She believed it all and began saying what the angel said to say. At one point she was led to a hotel room to spend extended time in prayer to and with the angel. During this "retreat," she was asked to have sexual relations with the angel, which she did. It was after this that the messages from the angel became increasingly dark and her own battle with depression took a huge turn for the worst. Because of her falling for *The Angel of Light Scheme*, she had opened many attachment points in her life to the work of evil spirits. She also was not making the positive difference that she had hoped to make.

What she was really seeking was a true spiritual experience with God the Father, God the Son, and God the Holy Spirit. I introduced her to the Lord Jesus Christ and he brought freedom from the growing darkness that was enveloping her life. It took many months to de-entangle her from the faulty thinking and heretical spiritual power that had captivated her. Her desire for a touch from the other side opened a door to the dark side of the spiritual realm that began to torment her. She fell for the Devil's *Angel of Light Scheme.*

Internal and External Versions

There are both internal and external versions of *The Angel of Light Scheme.* The internal aspect might be an angel (demon) appearing in dreams or speaking clearly into a person's mind. Usually the demon's instruction is to do something destructive or negative or to fill a person's mind with dark mental images. The way you can tell them apart is that God's messages are always holy and conform to the Word of God. God guides a person to repentance and not to a place of depression and condemnation.

Through this scheme some people are plagued by spiritual voices, messages given to them alone. Yes, there are psychological states where this phenomenon takes place; they are considered a form of mental illness. But there are also spiritual maladies where the Devil is running his *Angel of Light Scheme,* and it should be investigated. If the voices or dark images stem from a mental illness, then there is no particular reaction to reading the Bible, hearing the name of "Jesus," or singing worship songs. But if the condition is a spiritual malady because of the presence of an evil spirit, then there will be significant reaction to "Jesus Christ," reading the Bible, and singing worship songs. This makes sense for *God is light; in him there is no darkness at all, (1 John 1:5).*

An external manifestation would be an appearance of an angel to the individual or group. The wisdom might be shared through a medium speaking for a spirit. A medium might share hidden information to try and prove that they do have extraterrestrial wisdom. If we allow ourselves to be directed by a spiritual power or spiritual person which is not directed by the Lord Jesus Christ or the Word of God, then we could fall victim to *The Angel of Light Scheme.*

This scheme is not new. Look at what the Apostle Paul says in Galatians 1:6-8:

> *I am amazed that you are so quickly deserting Him who called you by the grace of Christ, for a different gospel; which is really not another gospel; only there are some who are disturbing you and want to distort the gospel of Christ. But even if we, or an angel from heaven, should preach to you a gospel contrary to what we have preached to you, he is to be accursed.*

Paul, speaking under the inspiration of the Holy Spirit, says that angels may come and try and distort the gospel or share a separate gospel. When this happens, the Apostle says that this is a cursed angel or a demon. This is *The Angel of Light Scheme.* There is one gospel. Lest we become confused about that, let's look at 1 Corinthians 15:1-5:

> *Now I make known to you, brethren, the gospel which I preached to you, which also you received, in which also you stand, by which also you are saved, if you hold fast the word which I preached to you, unless you believed in vain. For I delivered to you as of first importance what I also received, that Christ died for our sins according to the Scriptures, and that He was buried, and that He was raised on the third day according to the Scriptures, and that He appeared to Cephas, then to the twelve.*

The Galatian believers needed to remember that the good news of Christ is salvation that can't be earned. It is a free gift that none of us deserve. God has paid the price through his only begotten Son, Jesus Christ. It is something we can all receive: the gift of eternal life. There was a lot of spiritual deception and spiritual power being displayed that was trying to lead people astray from the simplicity of the gospel. Let's be sure that we aren't the ones who fall for it!

- Spiritual power must be holy or it is not true.

- Spiritual power must come from the Lord Jesus Christ and be focused on glorifying him if it is to be trusted.

- Spiritual power and wisdom must agree with the Word of God or it is accursed.

Lucifer

Let's now talk about the spiritual wisdom aspect of this scheme. This aspect can be coupled with spiritual power but not always. Satan presents "wisdom" that is beyond the natural or ordinary. It is often put in a context of secrets. Oftentimes it is nothing more than bits of information about individuals that would be unknown normally but are shared to convince the person that they are about to hear "wisdom" they should pay attention to. This is all a part of this *Angel of Light Scheme.* It is practiced in tarot card readings, séances, channeling, and the like. The Bible condemns this desire for hidden knowledge as wrong because spirits will always use it to lead you astray (Leviticus 19:26; Jeremiah 14:14; Jeremiah 29:8; Ezekiel 13:6). On a human level, this *Spiritual Power and Wisdom Scheme* is often just the work of conmen and charlatans to separate a person and their money; but when it is real spirits giving "wisdom," it is a part of this scheme.

This whole scheme grows out of who the Devil is and how he was supposed to give God glory. In Ezekiel 28:12-19, the origins of the Devil are described: he is given the name *Lucifer, the Son of the Morning, and the Son of the Dawn.* In

Hebrew this is the word *Helel*. It means "the morning star" or "the crescent moon." Lucifer was judged because of his rebellion, pride, and selfishness. He was removed from the exalted place he once held, but he still understands the power of beauty, display, and wisdom. He knows how to use beauty and logic for evil purposes.

> *Son of man, take up a lamentation over the king of Tyre and say to him, "Thus says the Lord GOD, You had the seal of perfection, Full of wisdom and perfect in beauty. You were in Eden, the garden of God; Every precious stone was your covering: The ruby, the topaz and the diamond; The beryl, the onyx and the jasper; The lapis lazuli, the turquoise and the emerald; And the gold, the workmanship of your settings and sockets, Was in you. On the day that you were created they were prepared. You were the anointed cherub who covers, And I placed you there. You were on the holy mountain of God; You walked in the midst of the stones of fire. You were blameless in your ways From the day you were created Until unrighteousness was found in you. By the abundance of your trade You were internally filled with violence, And you sinned; Therefore I have cast you as profane From the mountain of God. And I have destroyed you, O covering cherub, From the midst of the stones of fire. Your heart was lifted up because of your beauty; You corrupted your wisdom by reason of your splendor. I cast you to the ground; I put you before kings, That they may see you. By the multitude of your iniquities, In the unrighteousness of your trade You profaned your sanctuaries. Therefore I have brought fire from the midst of you; It has consumed you, And I have turned you to ashes on the earth In the eyes of all*

*who see you. All who know you among the peoples
Are appalled at you; You have become terrified And
you will cease to be forever." (Ezek. 28:12-19)*

In this part of *The Angel of Light Scheme,* the Devil uses
beauty and/or wisdom to lure people to their destruction.
This can mean using beauty and wisdom towards a sexual
end outside of marriage or using beauty and wisdom as an
end in and of itself. It can mean that conspiracy theories and
connections between groups and events that really don't exist
are made to seem to exist. Lucifer is capable of spinning tales
and making it all sound so logical; but it is a lie and if you
believe it, you have been consumed and your good works
have been left undone. Notice that the Scripture says that
Lucifer corrupted his beauty and corrupted his wisdom.
Therefore in this scheme, people are subjected to a corrupted
form of God's wisdom and beauty.

I can remember when a version of this scheme was being
tried against a group of us as we were praying for a young
lady; who was deeply oppressed by the Devil. As we prayed
for her and helped her walk out of the sins and deception that
were a part of her life, she began asking us if we wanted to
know about the sins of people in the church. We told her and
the spirit that was supplying the information, "NO!" We
didn't want her information. But the spirit would try and
sneak it in as we were working with her on other issues. Each
time; we refused to hear the gossip and slander about others,
and eventually, the woman was free from the demonic
presence and information.

The United States saw an extreme version of this scheme
being run through David Koresh at his cult farm in Waco,
Texas, in the 1990's. He convinced dozens of families to
leave everything and listen to him spin lies out of the Bible

and his head. This led to a deadly shoot out and the destruction of so many. If some "wisdom" sounds fishy, then it just may be; and you might want to move away from it. If no one but the spiritual authority you are hearing this from thinks this makes any sense, then it may not be true.

A common form of this *Angel of Light Scheme* is run through a number of "secret" ritualistic organizations that are in most major cities. I remember talking with one of my relatives who became enamored with the teachings of one of these secret organizations. He wanted to pledge to this organization and move up the levels in their structure. He liked the fact that they gave money for hospitals, but he was unwilling to look at what they actually taught about God. He felt spiritual power when he went to their meetings. Their "secret" knowledge and understandings were fascinating to him. He moved into this organization over my strong objections, and he never again considered the claims of Jesus Christ, the Savior of the World. He gave into *The Angel of Light Scheme.*

Who Is Influencing Us?

How do we make sure that we are not deceived by Satan in what we believe, in what we practice, in the spiritual feelings and gifts we accept, and in the promptings we are guided by? How do I authentically know that something or someone is from God?

We can find out the answer to these questions by running through four biblical tests that allow us to determine whether some spiritual power or wisdom display is from God or from some other source (often demonic).

120

1. **The first test is to look at the fruit of the ministry (Matt. 7:15-23).** What type of results does this ministry, person, or organization produce? Are they holy? Do they accomplish righteous things? Do the people themselves live righteous lives? Are there immorality and violations of God's laws allowed within the organization?

When someone comes to me and asks about a spiritual gift, experience, or healing they have had, I usually say, "That is wonderful!" Then I ask, "Since you have had this gift, experience, or healing, have you had an easier time being holy and free from sin or a harder time?" I am amazed at the number of times people tell me, "Funny you should mention that to me. Since I received this (gift), (experience), or (healing), I am having such a hard time resisting temptation." That should tell you something about the source right there.

2. **The second test is to look at the content of the message, the organization, and the person (1 Cor. 12:1-3).** What is actually being said by the person, in the meetings, by the spirit speaking in the tongue? Does it line up with the *whole counsel* of Scripture? It is not enough to just take one verse because it is possible to twist one verse to say some wacko idea. When the messages of the organization and/or the person is examined, what are they are actually saying about God, Jesus, the Holy Spirit, salvation, the afterlife, or the End Times? It is not sufficient to just mention Jesus a few times in a meeting and have it be orthodox. The truth of God comes out of the Word of God and agrees with the Word of God.

I will usually ask a question somewhat like this to get at this content test: "Since you have received this gift, experience, or healing, do you have a great desire to read and study the Bible or do you have less interest?" If a person is not interested in hearing and knowing more about the Bible from a spiritual experience or event, then something is not good. Even if a person is not a reader by nature, the Holy Spirit draws a person into the Bible. Find a mature Christian who knows their Bible and see if what is happening lines up with their understanding of the doctrines of Scripture.

3. **A third test that should be run on spiritual power and wisdom is to test the spirit itself.** The Apostle John says in 1 John 4:1-4,

> *Beloved, do not believe every spirit, but test the spirits to see whether they are from God, because many false prophets have gone out into the world. By this you know the Spirit of God: every spirit that confesses that Jesus Christ has come in the flesh is from God; and every spirit that does not confess Jesus is not from God; this is the spirit of the antichrist, of which you have heard that it is coming, and now it is already in the world. You are from God, little children, and have overcome them; because greater is He who is in you than he who is in the world.*

This usually requires a person with the gift of discernment of spirits to pray and see what is happening in the meeting or organization in the spiritual realm. It also is possible to have the spirits tested against the biblical question mentioned in the text: "Do you confess that Jesus Christ has come in the flesh?" A third way of testing the spirits in a spiritual experience, gift, or healing is to say openly,

"What do you think about the Lord Jesus Christ?" or "I believe in the Lord Jesus Christ" and then see what happens. If the room, the people, the organization, or the person is excited about the Lord Jesus Christ, then this is great! If not, it may be a *Spiritual Power and Wisdom Scheme*.

4. **The fourth biblical test is the test of the gospel or the Good News.** What is the gospel that this person or group is proclaiming? Every organization is trying to get a message out. What is this essential good news that is being proclaimed? If it is something other than the forgiveness of God that is available through Jesus Christ the Savior, then it is false good news. The Good News is *not* that you can have a spiritual experience; that you can be rich; that everything is predestined; that you can speak another language; or that God loves some people more than other people. The good news is *God so loved the whole world that He gave His only begotten Son, that whosoever believes in Him should not perish but have eternal life (John 3:16).* I referenced Galatians 1:6-8 earlier, but it is very appropriate here. Even if an angel presents a different gospel than the one of Jesus Christ's death on a cross for the sins of the world, it is wrong and that angel is an accursed angel.

I will ask a person, "Since you have received this gift, experience, or healing, do you have an easier time forgiving people or a harder time forgiving and overlooking people's faults?" Jesus tells us in Matthew 18 that when we really are aware of how much God has forgiven us, we must have a forgiving heart toward others who have offended us.

Jesus Instructs Us to "Watch Out!"

After Jesus rose from the dead and ascended into heaven, he came back to earth sixty years later to make sure that people do not fall victim to *The Angel of Light Scheme*. He appeared in a cave on the island of Patmos and gave a special revelation to the last surviving apostle, John. He wanted to tell all the Christians how history is going to end and to give an evaluation on how his church is doing. He picked out seven specific churches to commend, rebuke, correct, and encourage. His instructions almost always include a section about watching out for demonic deception. The church had let the Devil deceive them through false doctrine, false teachers, false prophets, false leaders, false phenomena, and false practices. Satan was running the *Angel of Light Scheme* and many of the churches were falling victim to it. Look at what Jesus says to the pastors and churches about the scheme that was being allowed in their churches.

Ephesus

I know your deeds and your toil and perseverance, and that you cannot tolerate evil men, and you put to the test those who call themselves apostles, and they are not, and you found them to be false; (Revelation 2:2)

Smyrna

I know your tribulation and your poverty (but you are rich), and the blasphemy by those who say they are Jews and are not, but are a synagogue of Satan. Do not fear what you are about to suffer. Behold, the Devil is about to cast some of you into prison, so that you will be tested, and you will have tribulation for ten days. Be

faithful until death, and I will give you the crown of life.
(Revelation 2:9,10)

Pergamum

I know where you dwell, where Satan's throne is; and
you hold fast My name, and did not deny My faith even
in the days of Antipas, My witness, My faithful one,
who was killed among you, where Satan dwells. But I
have a few things against you, because you have there
some who hold the teaching of Balaam, who kept
teaching Balak to put a stumbling block before the sons
of Israel, to eat things sacrificed to idols and to commit
acts of immorality. So you also have some who in the
same way hold the teaching of the Nicolaitans.
Therefore repent; or else I am coming to you quickly,
and I will make war against them with the sword of My
mouth. (Revelation 2:13-16)

Thyatira

'I know your deeds, and your love and faith and service
and perseverance, and that your deeds of late are greater
than at first. 'But I have this against you, that you
tolerate the woman Jezebel, who calls herself a
prophetess, and she teaches and leads My bond-servants
astray so that they commit acts of immorality and eat
things sacrificed to idols. I gave her time to repent, and
she does not want to repent of her immorality.
(Revelation 2:19-21)

But I say to you, the rest who are in Thyatira, who do
not hold this teaching, who have not known the deep

things of Satan, as they call them—I place no other burden on you. (Revelation 2:24)

Sardis

But you have a few people in Sardis who have not soiled their garments; and they will walk with Me in white, for they are worthy. (Revelation 3:4)

Philadelphia

I know your deeds. Behold, I have put before you an open door which no one can shut, because you have a little power, and have kept My word, and have not denied My name. Behold, I will cause those of the synagogue of Satan, who say that they are Jews and are not, but lie—I will make them come and bow down at your feet, and make them know that I have loved you. (Revelation 3:8,9)

Laodicea

Because you say, "I am rich, and have become wealthy, and have need of nothing," and you do not know that you are wretched and miserable and poor and blind and naked, I advise you to buy from Me gold refined by fire so that you may become rich, and white garments so that you may clothe yourself, and that the shame of your nakedness will not be revealed; and eye salve to anoint your eyes so that you may see. Those whom I love, I reprove and discipline; therefore be zealous and repent. (Revelation 3:17-19)

Just like we saw with Paul in his message to the church at Galatia, the Devil has sent false doctrine, deceiving spirits, false phenomena, false extreme practices, and false teachers to lure the church into error for two thousand years. He will continue to do this, and we must know how to discern truth and error. Remember, the church is the collection of all those who have embraced that Jesus Christ is the Son of God as Savior down through the centuries.

There is such an interest in spiritual experiences these days that good people will drive hundreds of miles to watch what seems like a righteous Christ-honoring service. They came to see something spiritual happen. The key question is; Who is sponsoring the spiritual power? It is possible that the spiritual power is coming from the wrong source. Remember these questions and ask when them when you are in the presence of a demonstration of spiritual power or are talking to someone who has had something spiritual happen to them.

- What is the fruit? (Matt. 7:15-23),
- What is the content? (1 Cor. 12:1-3)
- What is the spirit? (1 John 4:1-4)
- What is the gospel (good news) it proclaims? (Gal. 1:6-8)

People can easily be duped into following the signs, feelings, and the supernatural rather than God and his Word.

As a final warning, look at what Paul delivers in 2 Corinthians 11:3,

> *But I am afraid that, as the serpent deceived Eve by his craftiness, your minds will be led astray from the simplicity and purity of devotion to Christ.*

The aim of this scheme is to show us spiritual power or wisdom in order to distract us away from devotion to Jesus

Christ. There are some people who seem to preach and believe that you start with Jesus Christ as a Christian but then you graduate on to something better. This is not true. We start with Christ and we finish with Christ. Jesus is the door, and he is what we see when the door opens. God will one day sum up everything in Jesus. Do not be deceived by false, spiritual power (Phil. 2:5-10; Col. 1:13-20; 2:1-15).

Exercises to Defeat The Angel of Light

How do we defeat Satan as he and his demons run *The Angel of Light Scheme* against us? There are eight actions and spiritual antidotes that are known as the Armor of God that are essential to winning the life God has always wanted for you. They will be a crucial part of beating the opposition of Satan. Satan wants to destroy us and add us to his manure pile of wasted people, wasted skills, wasted opportunities, and wasted lives. But we can win the life that God has planned for us through Christ. God has given us all we need; we just have to start using all that he has provided.

These spiritual weapons are truth, righteousness, peace, faith, salvation, Word of God (God's Wisdom), prayer, and alertness. The Devil acts against these qualities because in order to destroy a life, he needs to distort or attack each of these. In every scheme, there is an attack against, or distortion of, one of these spiritual realities. It is these qualities that bring health, blessing, peace, and joy to people.

Let me write these again in a graphically interesting way so you will hopefully remember them. Memorize them. Use them. Write your own copy of them. Draw them. Embroider them. Ask God for insight on how to increase their use in your life. You and I will need these to defeat the Schemes of the Satan.

Truth

Righteousness

Peace

Faith

Salvation

Word of God

Prayer

Alertness

In these we have the answers, the antidotes, and the super-weapons that will defeat *The Angel of Light Scheme*. We also have the Holy Spirit guiding us as to which one to use at what time. Each of these spiritual weapons is a scheme buster, but we are to be guided by the Holy Spirit in our deployment of these weapons. We don't just use all the weapons every time we sense a spiritual attack; there are usually one or two that need our focus at a time. There are numerous examples in Scripture where the Holy Spirit directed people to use only one or two weapons instead of all of them (Matt. 4:1-12; Matt. 26:36-46). When I am under attack, I pray down through these spiritual weapons and ask God to guide me to just the right one for the spiritual power scheme I am facing.

Now it is important to note that the first three spiritual weapons are to be deployed constantly in your life. As the

Apostle Paul outlines, these spiritual weapons are distinct between the first three and the last five.

> Stand firm therefore, *HAVING GIRDED YOUR LOINS WITH TRUTH, and HAVING PUT ON THE BREASTPLATE OF RIGHTEOUSNESS, and having shod YOUR FEET WITH THE PREPARATION OF THE GOSPEL OF PEACE; in addition to all, taking up the shield of faith with which you will be able to extinguish all the flaming arrows of the evil one. And take THE HELMET OF SALVATION, and the sword of the Spirit, which is the word of God. With all prayer and petition pray at all times in the Spirit, and with this in view, be on the alert with all perseverance and petition for all the saints... (Eph. 6:14-18)*

Notice that for the first three, he uses the past tense verb *of having,* as in already in the past having put on these weapons: Truth, Righteousness, and Peace. You are always to be standing on truth and learning more. We are always to be righteous and loving. We are always to be peaceable and forgiving. The last five weapons are to be taken up and deployed when the battle rages: Faith, Salvation, Word of God, Prayer, and Alertness.

Engaging God in Your Spiritual Battle with the Angel of Light

Just as Jesus was completely dependent upon the Father and the Spirit, we are dependent upon the whole of the Trinity for our victory in the spiritual battles of our life. Too many Christians act like they are on there own when facing

Satan. They think God threw the manual (Bible) at them and told them, "Read it; all the answers are in there." God is with us and has prepared all the weapons, knows the right strategy, and will give us wisdom and guidance if we ask for it and expect to receive it. Seriously ask God in prayer the following questions when you think Satan is running *The Angel of Light Scheme.*

What spiritual weapon should I to use against *The Angel of Light Scheme?*

- Is it truth?
- Is it righteousness?
- Is it peace?
- Is it faith or God-ordained risk?
- Is it a God-provided way of escape or element of hope?
- Is it wisdom from God's Word?
- Is it prayer?
- Is it alertness and precaution?

Once you have answered these questions, then it is time to go deeper on the particular weapons you are supposed to deploy. In the exercises that follow I have made a lot of educated guesses about what you may need to defeat a particular scheme, but it is more important that you stay sensitive to the Lord Jesus as he guides you to the particular way of using the Armor of God to defeat the schemes of Satan. It is also very helpful to have a pastor, mentor, life coach, wise friend, or counselor help you understand how to defeat the enemy. When you are facing repeated opposition to good works and righteous ideas, internally ask these questions and act to protect yourself. Satan's opposition and enemies are tests of our resolve. God loves us and wants us to get through this test and be stronger on the other side. If you are going after some good thing, some righteous development then you can expect to have opposition and enemies. Satan is always trying to block us from the abundant life God has planned. Don't fall for it.

Further Questions to Ask

Pray down through these questions and let God the Holy Spirit guide you to the particular spiritual weapon that he wants you to deploy against *The Angel of Light Scheme.*

What **truth(s)** would stop *The Angel of Light Scheme* and deliver the individual, group, or nation?

- It may be truths about God that will win the day.
- It may be truths about Christian living that will win the day.
- It may be truths about ourselves that will win the day.
- It may be truths about others and/or society that will win the day.
- It may be a particular scientific fact or historical field that will dispel the deception and schemes of the enemy.

What **righteousness, love, or morality** would stop *The Angel of Light Scheme* and deliver the individual, group, or nation?

- It may be that you need to increase your love in one of the relationships of your life.
- It may be that you need to increase the wisdom of the love in one of your relationships.

- It may be that you need to do good and right things that you have not been doing.
- It may be that you need to stop doing some unloving, unrighteous, or damaging actions or words.
- It may be that you need to ask about an opportunity you are being given:
  • Will this actually do good? Will this harm others?

  • Is this really just about my desire and I am being led along by my desire?

What **peace moves** or strategies would stop *The Angel of Light Scheme* and deliver the individual, group, or nation?

- It may be that you need to make peace with God in ways that you haven't yet.
- It may be that you need to examine or lower your expectations or the anger will still win.
- It may be that you need to change some of your actions or the circumstances that surround the tense moments in your life.
- It may be that you need to forgive God, yourself, or others to defeat this scheme.
- It may be that you need to turn this enemy into a friend.
- It may be that you need to stop acting with hostility in a particular situation.
- It may be that you need to start positive steps to bring about peace with others.
- It may be that you need to leave all justice with God.
- It may be that you need more than just peace you need harmony with another person.

What **faith steps** or God-directed risks would stop *The Angel of Light Scheme* and deliver the individual, group, or nation?

- It may be that you need to trust God for something that is right but very hard to do.
- It may be that you need to learn more about God and the Christian life so that your trust is more solid and informed.
- It may be that God wants you to trust him and head in a new direction to defeat this particular scheme of the Devil.
- It may be that you need to decide to trust God when it doesn't feel like the best solution.
- It may be that you must trust God when you are making no progress as that is better than the progress toward the wrong goals.

What **ways of escape (salvation) or hope** would stop *The Angel of Light Scheme* and deliver the individual, group, or nation?

- It may be that you need to explore and take fuller advantage of the salvation that is in the Lord Jesus Christ than you have in the past.
- It may be that you are supposed to take some way of escape that will get you out of a situation that is too tempting, too pressurized, too dangerous, or too life altering for you.
- It may be that you must hold on to or look for the elements of hope from your past and in the present as you wait for God's deliverance.

- It may be that you have to cling to the hope of your salvation: the return of Christ and your place in heaven to say *no* to the temptations of the Devil in this life.

What **wisdom from God's Word** would stop *The Angel of Light Scheme* and deliver the individual, group, or nation?

- It may be that you need to read the Scriptures daily so that God can prompt you with the appropriate verses when you need them.
- It may be that you need to read through the Scriptures so that you have a grasp of what God is saying in the whole of the Word of God.
- It may be that you need to go to a class, seminar, or small group where you can get a better overview of the Old and New Testament.
- It may be that you need to learn how to study the Scriptures so that when God prompts you with a verse, you can study it and gain the appropriate understanding of what God is saying.
- It may be that you need to learn how to meditate on the Word of God so that when God gives you a Scripture, you know how to carry it around in your mind all day.
- It may be that you need to quote a verse of Scripture to yourself all day to defeat the scheme the Devil is running.
- It may be that you need to quote a particular verse of Scripture at the Devil to let him know that you are on to his scheme. You now know the wisdom of God and will not be fooled by his ideas and opportunities.

What **kind and type of prayers** would stop *The Angel of Light Scheme* and deliver the individual, group, or nation?

- It may be that God prompts you to spend time praising him as the antidote to a particular scheme of the Devil.
- It may be that God wants you to prayerfully contemplate a Scripture as the way to win against a particular scheme.
- It may be that God wants you to request certain things from him that you will need to win against this particular scheme.
- It may be that God wants you to pray for someone else to defeat this scheme.
- It may be that you need to pray prayers of gratefulness in order to pass the test that is being thrown at you.
- It may be that you need to confess your sins or the sins of the group or your nation in order to stop this scheme from succeeding.
- It may be that God wants you to battle for the unconverted soul(s) you know that need the Lord in order to defeat this particular scheme of the Devil.
- It may be that you need to pray for government officials that they would be safe and ethical as they make decisions and unthreatened by interests groups that are evil.

What **precautions and/or alertness** would stop *The Angel of Light Scheme* and deliver the individual, group, or nation?

- It may be that God wants you to make very specific preparations to withstand a scheme or test of the Devil.
- It may be that you have an exposed weakness to sin that will damage, dishonor, or destroy you if it is not dealt

with; and you must protect yourself and your loved ones in some way before the storm of the test arrives.

- It may be that you do not know enough about a crucial relationship or truth of Christianity and God is giving you the heads-up about learning how to make that right. You must act before the test comes, or it will hurt you or stop your progress.

Scheme #6

The Dragon Scheme
(Amplified Anger)

Hal was devoted to his family. He wanted to raise his children as Christians and do right by people. He married a younger woman, Amy, and they had four children. When his wife was close to forty years of age, she listened to some immoral friends who convinced her to use her beauty before it was gone for some fun outside of her marriage. She listened to the Devil's lure through them and began attending parties. She attracted the attention of many men. Hal worked hard to keep his marriage intact and to understand his wife. Eventually, Amy was getting so much attention and promises from younger and richer men that she filed for divorce. Nothing Hal could do convinced Amy to come back to him and their four children. Hal sunk into depression and bitterness, and he began to stew. "How could she do this to me?" "What will this do to the children?" On the day the divorce was final, Hal let the bitterness, anger, rage and depression get to him at a whole new level. He hadn't been to a bar and gotten drunk since he was in the military decades before, but he went that night. By the time the bar closed down, he was very drunk and made the mistake of getting behind the wheel. He wanted to get home to his children. Unfortunately he did not see the man who was crossing the street a short ways from the bar. He hit him full force and only saw him as his body slammed into the windshield. He had killed him. Hal was arrested and booked on vehicular homicide. The Devil had run *The Dragon Scheme* on Hal and it destroyed his life. Yes, it was awful what his wife did to them. Yes, it was not fair to the children that their mother abandoned them. But Hal gave into a temptation also—to nurse his anger, bitterness, and rage. This whole true story is tragic and it speaks to how the Devil will run various schemes against us to destroy the good we are doing and could do in the future.

The Devil likes to amplify emotions and get you to act in ways that are emotionally driven and unwise. Actions and words said in the embrace of strong emotion can do great damage and you can't take them back. This particular scheme is about the amplification of anger that builds until you resort to abuse, vengeance, violence, and even murder. Unresolved anger gives a place to the Devil as few emotions do (Eph. 4:26,27).

The Devil is called the Dragon because of the terror, power, and rage he displays. The Devil will seek to tempt us into becoming a Dragon through anger, bitterness, violence, and rage or wilting under its hot blasts and abandoning God's direction in our life. When he is running the *Dragon scheme,* anger is always involved. Notice in the following passage that the Devil is called the Dragon in the midst of war. He is trying to assert his dominance, control, and will through anger, violence,and murder.

Revelation 12:7-9 - *And there was war in heaven, Michael and his angels waging war with the **dragon**. The **dragon** and his angels waged war, and they were not strong enough, and there was no* *longer a place found for them in heaven. And the great **dragon** was thrown down, the serpent of old who is called the Devil and Satan, who deceives the whole world; he was thrown down to the earth, and his angels were thrown down with him.*

In the above passage the Devil is referred to as the *dragon*. This is a transliterated Greek word d-r-a-g-o-n using the Greek letters in English to describe the idea of a monstrous, multi-headed, winged creature reigning terror on those it comes against. The picture is the war between the holy angels and the angels of darkness in the initial rebellion of Satan. Satan uses amplified anger and terror to destroy the good. He wants to exert his dominance and will over the angels, over people, and the world as a whole. He becomes a dragon when his rage, selfishness, and violence flashes out against those who oppose him. In the same way he tempts people to go down that same path of using amplified anger to get their way, to exert their dominance. We see this with domestic violence, with human trafficking, with child abuse, and with war. Someone is becoming the dragon and using anger, violence, and power to exert control.

The Scriptures consistently exhort us to not give into anger because it so rarely produces any good in its raw form. It is normal to feel anger but do not be seduced into using anger to accomplish your goals or you will become a dragon to those around you. James 1:19 reads: *This you know, my beloved brethren. But everyone must be quick to hear, slow to speak and slow to anger.* We must be careful that we do not allow the Devil to tempt us into becoming a dragon through anger, rage, bitterness or malice.

Anger is a unique emotion in that it so quickly moves a person to action. It is raw, emotional fuel; and if it is not handled properly, it can be so destructive, so violent, and so deadly. We all experience anger from time to time. It's a normal emotion. In fact, anger is not from the Devil at all but the *amplification* of anger can be. Amplified anger can kill even though no one physically dies. Anger can kill one's relationships and future through choices, decisions, and actions made in the midst of rage. Anger can induce a person to use their car as an extension of their anger and produce an accident or compel a person to say or scream words that can never be taken back. The Devil loves to use anger as the emotional context to suggest more extreme actions and words than a person would ever use on their own. In the swirling winds of anger, actions, words, and ideas can seem right that in a calmer frame of mind would never be embraced.

In this *Dragon Scheme*, the Devil will amplify the normal anger that rises in us when things don't go our way until it seems like we must act. We must speak our mind. We must scheme to get back at the person. We feel compelled to do something against the person, group, or organization that caused us so much pain. At times the anger, bitterness, or rage can be overwhelming. Like blowing wind over a small fire, the Devil seeks to whip it into a raging inferno in our minds until it must break out with words and actions. Sometimes the Devil will send the angry, enraged person at you. His goal in all these versions of *The Dragon Scheme* is for you to stop doing something you are doing or planning to do. He wants you to not take the steps you are about to take.

Related Scriptures

Let's take a look at the Scriptures in regard to this scheme:

> *BE ANGRY, AND yet DO NOT SIN; do not let the sun go down on your anger, and do not give the Devil an opportunity. (Ephesians 4:26,27)*

Anger is not wrong; it is natural. The Bible says that anger should not continue to exist in your soul in its raw form. Anger must be processed into fuel for positive change, or it will become destructive to your life. Anger is the evidence that something is wrong or at least not the way we would want it. But anger is such a strong emotion that it must be processed and not allowed to fester in our soul lest it create a problem. Eventually, the Devil whispers, "Do you want some help in being angry?" In this way he seeks to establish a foothold, a base of operation. All he has to do to keep you from doing something righteous or loving is to stir up your anger over some inconsequential thing and you will run right past the good work you could have done. I have worked with too many people who have allowed anger to be a part of their life, and it has given a place for the Devil to work all kinds of problems into their lives.

> *Never pay back evil for evil to anyone. Respect what is right in the sight of all men. If possible, so far as it depends on you, be at peace with all men. Never take your own revenge, beloved, but leave room for the wrath of God, for it is written, "VENGEANCE IS MINE, I WILL REPAY," says the Lord. "BUT IF YOUR ENEMY IS HUNGRY, FEED HIM, AND IF HE IS THIRSTY, GIVE HIM A DRINK; FOR IN SO DOING YOU WILL HEAP BURNING COALS ON HIS HEAD." Do not be overcome by evil, but overcome evil with good. (Rom. 12:17-21)*

One of the things that we have to recognize about anger is that it may exist inside a person's head as schemes of revenge. These ideas of vengeance and payback are clearly outlawed by God because they cloud the mind and give place to the

Devil. God warns us not to nurse vengeance, as it is too strong for us. God can handle any vengeance that needs to be administered and we cannot. The Devil loves to hide anger inside of our justified wrongs and desire for vengeance. It is not wrong to seek justice so that others are not hurt also, but we are to leave justice in the hands of God and his appointed representatives. The Devil can play too many tricks on us if we seek our own justice against those who hurt our loved ones or us personally.

*You are of your father the Devil, and you want to do the desires of your father. He was a **murderer** from the beginning, and does not stand in the truth because there is no truth in him. Whenever he speaks a lie, he speaks from his own nature, for he is a liar and the father of lies. (John 8:44)*

Jesus calls the Devil a *murderer* from the beginning. Jesus knows the Devil's history and saw him trick Cain into murder and how he encouraged Moses to deliver God's people through murder. Jesus knows that the Devil will use anger, vengeance, and violence to justify murder of a relationship, an organization, a racial group, a religious group, a person who is different, and a thousand other excuses to eliminate what gets in the way of our selfish wants. If someone is using violence or threats of violence against you to control you, then you are experiencing a form of this *Dragon Scheme*. It is a spiritual attack as well as a mental, emotional, and physical one. This is the end game of the Devil in this scheme. He is a murderer, so he wants to kill something whether it is your future, an important relationship, a job, an actual person, or an organization. He wants good works stopped and good people blocked from being good. Don't fall for this scheme.

Be angry but do not sin by giving yourself over to the selfishness of your anger.

In this scheme the Devil suggests that anger, violence, and the threat of violence are the answers to your problems. He may even suggest you murder a person. Sometimes he just wants you to mentally rehearse hurting, harming, or destroying the person you are at odds with. Realize that mentally picturing immoral actions is not good. It is not a good idea to mentally rehearse how you will get back at your enemies. It plants a pathway that makes action easier. It provides a selfish mental pathway instead of the righteous mental pathway that you could be thinking about. The Devil wants to see if a person will embrace any level of anger, vengeance, violence, and/or murder and induce them to action.

For some people this anger, vengeance, violence, and/or murder solution is always present. They just think to themselves that if they just eliminate the person, the problems will go away. Then they aren't around to stop you! The Devil wants to move them through violence, the threats of violence, or outright murder.

As we are descending more deeply into a post-Christian world, *The Dragon Scheme* will be more and more useful to the Devil. We have seen more husbands who are convinced that the only way to make a statement about the unfairness of a divorce settlement is to kill his ex-wife and children. This is *The Dragon Scheme* of the Devil being run inside the head of that father. There is surely life on the other side of the divorce, but the amplified anger and bitterness does not let them see it and they act. We are seeing this same scenario with disgruntled employees who are terminated and then allow the anger and bitterness to be amplified to the place

145

where they translate their emotions into the use of guns, knives, bombs, and usually suicide. These people became convinced in the swirl of angry emotions that there was no life on the other side of this job, and they needed to exact revenge.

This same *Dragon Scheme* is what is fueling the revenge porn outbreak where jilted boyfriends nurse their anger at their ex-girlfriend and share intimate photos on the Internet to get back at them. This makes no sense except under the influence of amplified anger. Teenagers now have new ways of "killing" their classmates through social media sites. We have already seen numerous people in the gall of bitterness and desire for revenge destroy others through posts and tweets on social media sites. When anger is amplified, it can justify all sorts of damaging, destructive, and deadly actions.

Internal and External Versions

As with all of these satanic schemes, there are both internal versions and external versions. If the Devil is running an internal version of *The Dragon Scheme* against us, he will take an injustice, a slight, or unmet expectation that would naturally produce anger or bitterness and seek to amplify that until the emotion has hijacked our rationality and wisdom. He doesn't need you to actually become violent or scream, although he would welcome that; all he needs you to do is continually nurse the anger and bitterness mentally. If he can get you to scheme against another or embrace a victim mentality, then that is sufficient to hijack your righteous future, and in many cases, change your present significantly.

There are also a number of ways the Devil can run an external version of this scheme. If this is the case, he can send someone into your life who will push a number of your anger buttons to see if he can engender in you enough anger to change your thinking about the future. He may have a person who is already in your life beginning to act differently toward you in ways that develop bitterness, anger, or significant frustration. This also would be to get you to focus on how wrong their actions are and fan into a flame your anger or bitterness at them. If that takes place, then he can amplify those feelings (if you do not resolve them) and begin to change your thinking and decision-making. Remember, the Devil's goal is to stop you from living out the righteous abundant life that Christ has planned for you.

Another way that the Devil may run an external *Dragon Scheme* on you is by having you become the carrier of the irritation, anger, and/or vengeance against another person. In this version of the scheme, you become aware of ways that you can push others' buttons; or if you are pushing their buttons and instead of stopping or trying for harmony, you just keep on doing the damaging things. It may produce internal or external anger in the other person, but all the while you become a willing participant in evil against another person. Remember, God tells us in Romans 12:17-21 that as far as it depends upon us, we are to be at peace with all men. We are to leave all vengeance and issues of justice to God and his duly constituted agents.

The Evil One

The Bible gives the Devil the title *The Evil One* in Matthew 13:19, John 17:15, and Ephesians 6:16. This title is composed of the Greek word *ponerous* and means "evil, one who does harm." The Merriam Webster's English dictionary defines evil as "causing harm or injury to someone." Evil is promoting gains that result in another's damage. It is not just that you want what you want but that you are presented with an opportunity to get what you want with the knowledge or fact that others will have to be damaged or destroyed in order for you to receive the gain you want. It is this damage to others that makes an action evil. It is the damage that is the evil, but our society must come to grips with the fact that millions of people will choose to damage others if they get what they want. That is the evil that lurks inside all of us. It is this extreme selfishness that the Devil exploits through amplified anger leading to vengeance, violence, and murder.

One of the things we must look at in this *Amplified Anger Scheme* is how destructive and harmful evil always becomes. Anger is often the fuel that allows evil to be accomplished. People who want to do evil often need anger to enrage them to destroy others. There are people who can do evil to others without anger. They have a hardened conscience, but they most likely started doing evil under the impulse of anger. Therefore, if people will eliminate the fuel (anger), they will hold themselves back from giving in to the promptings to be evil. Evil is a parasite on the good. Evil twists what is good for some greedy, pleasurable, egoistic, or power purpose. Evil means crossing the line between righteous gaining (where everyone gains) and gain at others' expense or destruction. Notice how the Devil hides the truth from people through evil (Matt. 13:19, Eph. 6:16).

There are people who have given themselves to The Evil One by being willing to do anything to others as long as they get what they want. What they are doing may even be couched in respectable terms within their context, but essentially they are choosing to damage or destroy others to get what they want when there are other options available. That is evil. "Why do you care what happens to them?" is The Evil One's stock reply. We should respond that what happens to others is always a part of a righteous person's life. Cain had the same evil attitude about his brother, Abel, when God called him out for the evil he did (Gen. 4:9). The thought, "I got what I wanted and I don't care who gets hurt in the process" is the flow of this thinking and scheme when it moves forward.

At some point in this *Dragon Scheme*, the end goal of doing evil does not even need to be masked by the emotions of anger, injustice, vengeance, or bitterness; the evil can be embraced for its selfishness. It says, "You are in my way and I want you out of my way. I want what you have, and I am willing to do anything to get what I want from you." This is why the Ten Commandments condemn murder, lying, stealing, adultery, and coveting.

I remember helping a woman we will call Margret pick up the pieces of her life. Her older brother, who we will call John, had just ended a long-term sexual relationship with her. In order to satisfy his growing, sexual appetites, John told Margret that he loved her as he continued to rape her through their teenage years. He promised her that they would always be together. John was the vessel that Satan used to deceive this woman and persuaded her to give her heart to this perverted relationship. She was fractured when the relationship finally ended. John had found another woman to fall for his web of deceit. He destroyed his sister to get what he wanted and he didn't care—this is the evil I'm talking about. In a very real way this man "murdered" his sister. Margret would never be the same after their "relationship" was over. As a part of her therapy she confronted him and he acted like it was not his problem what happened to her. His callousness was amazing. He was evil to his core, pretending to be righteous. He did not think anything of destroying other people as long as he got what he wanted.

Satan loves respectability covering over an evil core. The Devil can "murder" lots of people with agents like this. God substantially redeemed this woman and offered her significant healing and a solid marriage relationship later in life after much counseling and therapy. She married a very stable and patient man who was very different than her brother. He was a gift of God's grace to her. But the scars of what John did remain on her soul. Remember that you may be facing this *Amplified Anger Scheme* if you keep getting suggestions to get ahead by harming others.

Exercises to Defeat The Dragon Scheme

How do we defeat the Devil as he uses *The Dragon Scheme* to amplify anger, bitterness, vengeance, violence, and murder in us? There are eight actions and spiritual antidotes known as the Armor of God that are essential to winning the life God has always wanted for you. They will be a crucial part of beating the temptations of the Devil. The Devil wants to destroy us and add us to his manure pile of wasted people, wasted skills, wasted opportunities, and wasted lives. But we can win the life that God has planned for us through Christ. God has given us all we need; we just have to start using all that he has provided.

These spiritual weapons are truth, righteousness, peace, faith, salvation, Word of God (God's Wisdom), prayer, and alertness. The Devil acts against these qualities because in order to destroy a life, he needs to distort or attack each of these. In every scheme there is an attack against, or distortion of, one of these spiritual realities. It is these qualities that bring health, blessing, peace, and joy to people.

Let me write these again in a graphically interesting way so you will hopefully remember them. Memorize them. Use them. Write your own copy of them. Draw them. Ask God for insight on how to increase their use in your life. You and I will need these to defeat the Schemes of the Devil.

Truth

Righteousness

Peace

Faith

Salvation

Word of God

Prayer

Alertness

With these weapons we have the answers, the antidotes, and the super-weapons that will defeat amplified anger, bitterness, vengeance, violence, and murder. We also have the Holy Spirit guiding us as to which one to use at what time. Each of these spiritual weapons is a scheme buster, but we are to be guided by the Holy Spirit in our deployment of them. We don't just use all the weapons every time we sense a spiritual attack; there are usually one or two that need our focus at a time. There are numerous examples in Scripture where the Holy Spirit directed people to use only one or two weapons instead of all of them (Matt. 4:1-12; Matt. 26:36-46). When I am under attack, I pray down through these spiritual weapons and ask God to guide me to just the right one for any amplified anger I am facing, whether it is, bitterness, vengeance, violence, or murderous feelings.

Now it is important to note that the first three spiritual weapons are to be deployed constantly in your life. As the Apostle Paul outlines, these spiritual weapons are distinct between the first three and the last five.

> *Stand firm therefore, HAVING GIRDED YOUR LOINS WITH TRUTH, and HAVING PUT ON THE BREASTPLATE OF RIGHTEOUSNESS, and having shod YOUR FEET WITH THE PREPARATION OF THE GOSPEL OF PEACE; in addition to all, taking up the shield of faith with which you will be able to extinguish all the flaming arrows of the evil one. And take THE HELMET OF SALVATION, and the sword of the Spirit, which is the word of God. With all prayer and petition pray at all times in the Spirit, and with this in view, be on the alert with all perseverance and petition for all the saints, (Eph. 6:14-18).*

Notice that for the first three, he uses the past tense verb *of having*, as in already in the past having put on these weapons: Truth, Righteousness, and Peace. You are always to be standing on truth and learning more. We are always to be righteous and loving. We are always to be peaceable and forgiving. The last five weapons are to be taken up and deployed when the battle rages: Faith, Salvation, Word of God, Prayer, and Alertness.

Engaging God in Your Spiritual Battle with The Evil One

Just as Jesus was completely dependent upon the Father and the Spirit, we are dependent upon the whole of the Trinity for our victory in the spiritual battles of our life. Too many Christians act like they are on their own when facing the Devil. They think God threw the manual (Bible) at them and told them, "Read it; all the answers are in there." God is with us and has prepared all the weapons, knows the right strategy, and will give us wisdom and guidance if we ask for it and expect to receive it. Seriously ask God the following questions when you think the Devil is tempting, testing, or scheming against you.

What spiritual weapon should I to use against **amplified anger, bitterness, vengeance, violence, or murder?**

- Is it truth?
- Is it righteousness?
- Is it peace?
- Is it faith or God-ordained risk?
- Is it a God-provided way of escape or element of hope?
- Is it wisdom from God's Word?
- Is it prayer?
- Is it alertness and precaution?

Once you have answered these questions, then it is time to go deeper on the particular weapons you are supposed to deploy. In the exercises that follow I have made a lot of educated guesses about what you may need to defeat a particular scheme, but it is more important that you stay sensitive to the Lord Jesus as he guides you to the particular way of using the Armor of God to defeat the schemes of Satan. It is also very helpful to have a pastor, mentor, life coach, wise friend, or counselor help you understand how to defeat the enemy. When you are facing repeated instances of amplified anger and/or violence, ask these questions and act to protect yourself. The Dragon wants to inject us with his level of hatred and anger to push us off the path of Christ. God loves us and wants us to get through this test and be stronger on the other side. If it sounds too good to be true, it probably is. If everybody else is saying that this group or theory is wrong, then it has a chance of being wrong. The Devil is always leading away from the abundant life God has planned. Don't fall for it.

Further Questions to Ask

Pray down through these questions and let God the Holy Spirit guide you to the particular spiritual weapon that he wants you to deploy against amplified anger, bitterness, vengeance, violence, or murder?

What **truth(s)** would stop **amplified anger, bitterness, vengeance, violence, or murder** and deliver the individual, group, or nation?

- It may be truths about God that will win the day.
- It may be truths about Christian living that will win the day.
- It may be truths about ourselves that will win the day.
- It may be truths about others and/or society that will win the day.
- It may be a particular scientific fact or historical field that will dispel the deception and schemes of the enemy.

What **righteousness, love, or morality** would stop **amplified anger, bitterness, vengeance, violence, or murder** and deliver the individual, group, or nation?

- It may be that you need to increase your love in one of the relationships of your life.
- It may be that you need to increase the wisdom of the love in one of your relationships.
- It may be that you need to do good and right things that you have not been doing.
- It may be that you need to stop doing some unloving, unrighteous, or damaging actions or words.
- It may be that you need to ask about an opportunity you are being given:
  - Will this actually do good? Will this harm others?
  - Is this really just about my desire and I am being led along by my desire?

What **peace moves** or strategies would stop **amplified anger, bitterness, vengeance, violence, or murder** and deliver the individual, group, or nation?

- It may be that you need to make peace with God in ways that you haven't yet.
- It may be that you need to examine or lower your expectations or the anger will still win.
- It may be that you need to change some of your actions or the circumstances that surround the tense moments in your life.
- It may be that you need to forgive God, yourself, or others to defeat this scheme.
- It may be that you need to turn this enemy into a friend.

- It may be that you need to stop acting with hostility in a particular situation.
- It may be that you need to start positive steps to bring about peace with others.
- It may be that you need to leave all justice with God.
- It may be that you need more than just peace you need harmony with another person.

What **faith steps** or God-directed risks would stop **amplified anger, bitterness, vengeance, violence, or murder** and deliver the individual, group, or nation?
- It may be that you need to trust God for something that is right but very hard to do.
- It may be that you need to learn more about God and the Christian life so that your trust is more solid and informed.
- It may be that God wants you to trust him and head in a new direction to defeat this particular scheme of the Devil.
- It may be that you need to decide to trust God when it doesn't feel like the best solution.
- It may be that you must trust God when you are making no progress as that is better than the progress toward the wrong goals.

What **ways of escape (salvation) or hope** would stop **amplified anger, bitterness, vengeance, violence, or murder** and deliver the individual, group, or nation?

- It may be that you need to explore and take fuller advantage of the salvation that is in the Lord Jesus Christ than you have in the past.
- It may be that you are supposed to take some way of escape that will get you out of a situation that is too tempting, too pressurized, too dangerous, or too life altering for you.
- It may be that you must hold on to or look for the elements of hope from your past and in the present as you wait for God's deliverance.
- It may be that you have to cling to the hope of your salvation: the return of Christ and your place in heaven to say *no* to the temptations of the Devil in this life.

What **wisdom from God's Word** would stop **amplified anger, bitterness, vengeance, violence, or murder** and deliver the individual, group, or nation?

- It may be that you need to read the Scriptures daily so that God can prompt you with the appropriate verses when you need them.
- It may be that you need to read through the Scriptures so that you have a grasp of what God is saying in the whole of the Word of God.
- It may be that you need to go to a class, seminar, or small group where you can get a better overview of the Old and New Testament.
- It may be that you need to learn how to study the Scriptures so that when God prompts you with a verse, you can study it and gain the appropriate understanding of what God is saying.

- It may be that you need to learn how to meditate on the Word of God so that when God gives you a Scripture, you know how to carry it around in your mind all day.
- It may be that you need to quote a verse of Scripture to yourself all day to defeat the scheme the Devil is running.
- It may be that you need to quote a particular verse of Scripture at the Devil to let him know that you are on to his scheme. You now know the wisdom of God and will not be fooled by his ideas and opportunities.

What **kind and type of prayers** would stop **amplified anger, bitterness, vengeance, violence, or murder** and deliver the individual, group, or nation?

- It may be that God prompts you to spend time praising him as the antidote to a particular scheme of the Devil.
- It may be that God wants you to prayerfully contemplate a Scripture as the way to win against a particular scheme.
- It may be that God wants you to request certain things from him that you will need to win against this particular scheme.
- It may be that God wants you to pray for someone else to defeat this scheme.
- It may be that you need to pray prayers of gratefulness in order to pass the test that is being thrown at you.
- It may be that you need to confess your sins or the sins of the group or your nation in order to stop this scheme from succeeding.
- It may be that God wants you to battle for the unconverted soul(s) you know that need the Lord in order to defeat this particular scheme of the Devil.

- It may be that you need to pray for government officials that they would be safe and ethical as they make decisions and unthreatened by interests groups that are evil.

What **precautions and/or alertness** would stop **amplified anger, bitterness, vengeance, violence, or murder** and deliver the individual, group, or nation?

- It may be that God wants you to make very specific preparations to withstand a scheme or test of the Devil.
- It may be that you have an exposed weakness to sin that will damage, dishonor, or destroy you if it is not dealt with; and you must protect yourself and your loved ones in some way before the storm of the test arrives.
- It may be that you do not know enough about a crucial relationship or truth of Christianity and God is giving you the heads-up about learning how to make that right. You must act before the test comes, or it will hurt you or stop your progress.

Scheme #7

The Underworld Scheme
(Amplified Sin)

His name was Jim and he was twenty-one years old. Jim had just started attending our church, and he wanted to follow Christ. He also wanted to follow his dream of a musical career and was a talented enough musician to get a music contract and tour as the front act for a popular music group. But he knew what the music industry did to him. It tempted him to live a party life full of booze, sex, and drugs. So he chose to put off that lifestyle to try and have a meaningful relationship and close connection with Christ. He did well for a while, but then a new music promoter who had seen his previous work began talking with him, tempting him with another contract. This time it was for real money. He resisted, yet kept listening to the offer. I really thought he had won against the temptation, but he listened one more time to the promoter's offer. The next thing I knew he was gone. He had been lured back into the underground world of excessive partying that had no rules and no real relationships. Jim had fallen victim to *The Underworld Scheme.*

The Underworld Scheme is the Devil's attempt to attack you by exposing you to underworld behaviors, underworld associates, and/or underworld powers. His desire is to get you to embrace this manure-pile world as your own. He wants your dreams and goals to be confined to a trash heap of trouble. There are underworlds in every city. It is a world made up of perversion, crime, abuse, poverty, and hatred. Some of the underworlds consist of prostitution, organized crime, drug abuse, alcoholism, pornography, corrupt politicians, the occult and Satanism, gangs, drifters, and conmen. Each of these underworlds are perversions of normal life and are truly dog-eat-dog worlds where new moralities form around selfishness as the primary ethic.

Satan may send alluring images of the underworld into your dreams or into your thoughts. Whichever type and kind of underworld you are closest to or the one you might be the most susceptible to trying, will be brought across your path. He may bring a person into your life that is completely enmeshed in a version of the underworld at school, work, the gym, or even church. His goal is for you to strike up a friendship with someone who can introduce you to an underworld. Remember, that at first every underworld is exciting and pleasurable. There are no rules, no taboos, and a freedom to be selfish. The rules of the regular world of morality don't apply there. But after some time -- perhaps six months to a year later -- the consequences of the underworld come calling and demand payment.

Edith was a wonderful wife and mother until she took the job down at the local store to earn a little extra money for the family. The local market was really a glorified 7-11 with a gas station connected, and it was the only grocery store for our whole town. What Edith didn't know was that when she went to work, there were a lot of other people who worked there that were part of various underworlds. She made a friend at the store, Connie, who filled her with flattery about how beautiful she was and that her skills and beauty were wasted on her husband and family. Edith should come with her to some of the parties she went so she could see what real fun was all about. At first Edith declined. But then Edith agreed to go but just observed. Eventually Edith began to listen to the flattery and offers of drinks from the men at these parties that Connie always seemed to know about. Soon, the boring life of staying at home and helping the kids do homework and watching TV with her husband was not the life she wanted. Edith wanted the parties and the attention that came from the life that Connie had introduced her to.

After multiple affairs, Edith and her husband had some powerful decisions to consider. I remember sitting across from them as they debated whether to give their marriage another go or if she was going to run after the party scene that Connie had shown her. I told Edith that it all looked exciting now but that in less than five years, she would be beaten, raped, poor, and alone if she gave into the party scene. It was not worth it. I implored her to choose her wonderful family, her two girls, and her husband who was willing to take her back. I explained that when the life she was chasing after was done with her in a few years, her husband would most likely not want her back.

Unfortunately, Edith chose Connie's world over the stable world of her marriage. She ran off with a man she met at a party and lived with him for a few years until he beat her so bad she had to run away. Then she picked up with another man for a while and then another. About five years later she came back from her world of partying having aged twenty years, fighting various diseases she had picked up from Connie's exciting life, and she was alone. She went back to work at the store, but she was alone. Her husband had divorced her and remarried, and her children despised her for leaving during their teen years and for what she did to their dad. Edith chose the manure pile because it looked so exciting at first but then was stuck living on top of it for the rest of her life. No matter how many times I offered her repentance and forgiveness in Jesus Christ, her pride could not accept it because it would mean that I had been right all those years before.

Beelzebub

In Matthew 12:24 Jesus refers to the Devil as Beelzebub, which is a corruption of the name given to Baal in the Old Testament. In the original usage and spelling the name means Lord of the Underworld and Lord of the Spirits and Souls of the Underworld. This idea was stretched into the idea that Satan was the ruler of hell and controlled the fate of the wicked angels and wicked human souls. This theory was thoroughly debunked by Donald G. Barnhouse and many others. The Bible says that the Devil is not in hell; he is roaming to and fro across the earth tempting, testing, and bringing trials to everyone God will give him access to (Job 1). The Devil is not confined in the bottomless pit until after Jesus returns, not before (Rev. 20:1-3, 7-10). And the Devil does not rule in the bottomless pit; he will be a captive there and then judged in the lake of fire (Rev. 20:10).

Jesus corrupts the title Beelzebub, Lord of the Underworld, and calls the Devil the Lord of the Flies or the Lord of the Manure Pile. Yes, the Devil has followers -- both humans and spirits -- but it is not prestigious to follow him. He rules over the most undesirable territory. Jesus agrees that the Devil is the Lord of the demons, but he declares that these wicked spirits are like flies that rule over the refuse pile. Those people who give themselves over to refuse or manure-pile living are ruled by the wicked spirits who report back to the Devil.

We learn a number of things from Jesus's reference here. First, we learn that the worship of Baal from the past was really worship of the Devil. We learn that Baal and his consort, Ashtoreth, were the Lords of the Underworld as they claimed to be. But the Underworld was not a place of power; it was a place of judgment on their choices. When a person chooses an underworld life -- even if they are lured there -- then they have chosen to worship the god of the underworld. Just as in Baal worship of the past, those who embrace this lifestyle glory in their shame. They glory in abusing their children. They glory in perverted practices of sexuality. They glory in exalting spiritual powers other than God. They glory in betrayal and deceit. They glory in drug and alcohol abuse. They glory in stealing the innocence and purity of youth.

This god was nothing more than the Devil dressed up to look like the Lord of the Underworld when he really was in charge of the huge pile of moral filth that he had begun in the world. People worshipped selfish pleasure, the freedom to do damage to others, the degradation of themselves and their children; but they were really just adding to the Devil's manure pile. The Devil is the one who is in charge of the corruption of angels and mankind. He oversees the corruption, seeks to expand that corruption, and feeds on it. The Devil is in charge of those who keep failing his tests and temptations for moral purity, and they more and more give themselves over to self-focused pleasure. The debauchery gets deeper and deeper. Beelzebub creates more underworld living so more people can be sucked away from a life of meaning and purpose.

In this *Underworld Scheme*, the Devil shows that he is in charge of and feeds off of moral filth and excrement of people's evil choices. These underworlds are the remains and consequences of selfishness, sin, rebellion, and bitterness.

They are created by the practice of sin. Notice what the Apostle John says,

> *The one who practices sin is of the Devil; for the Devil has sinned from the beginning. The Son of God appeared for this purpose, to destroy the works of the Devil. No one who is born of God practices sin, because His seed abides in him; and he cannot sin, because he is born of God. By this the children of God and the children of the Devil are obvious: anyone who does not practice righteousness is not of God, nor the one who does not love his brother. For this is the message which you have heard from the beginning, that we should love one another; not as Cain, who was of the evil one and slew his brother. And for what reason did he slay him? Because his deeds were evil, and his brother's were righteous.* (1 John 3:8-12)

The Devil is king of a very disgusting hill. His hill grows with the refuse of the wasted lives of people who choose to please themselves at the expense of others. It grows with the actions of people who can only think about their own agenda and their own pleasure. Crawling over the dunghill of moral filth, they celebrate that they are living great lives when all they are really doing is destroying more of their limited time on earth and pulling others onto it with them.

> *If Satan casts out Satan, he is divided against himself; how then will his kingdom stand? If I by **Beelzebub** cast out demons, by whom do your sons cast them out? For this reason they will be your judges.* (Matt. 12:26,27)

In this *Underworld Scheme*, the Devil tests a person by offering garbage dressed up as something desirable. He makes drunken orgies seem exciting instead of demeaning rape parties and sexually transmitted disease supersites. He makes slave-like working conditions seem normal to accumulate profits and stock success. He makes dirty hotel rooms and drug dens seem like the right place to be to get your desires fulfilled. He makes gang initiations and senseless violence seem worthy of effort and endurance. He suggests that mob life is glamorous and not servile, senseless, and soul-deadening. He makes you believe that you can find meaning at the bottom of a bottle or by looking at one more picture of a naked woman you will never meet.

This *Underworld Scheme* is one of the basic roles of the Devil now. God has commissioned him as one of the beings that brings the consequences for sin. There are natural consequences of sin like disease, broken relationships, and missed opportunities. There are spiritual consequences like excessive emotional sensitivities, attachment of wicked spirits, and whispers to behave even more foolishly. The Devil as Beelzebub is the "excrement committee." After a person has sold their soul through a choice or a series of them, he comes to deliver the bad news. Beelzebub will induce you to repeatedly choose to sell your soul for a momentary pleasure and will pull you down to where you occupy a place on the manure pile with no thought of getting off except to move up, over, or down in position on the pile itself.

This scheme runs tests to draw you into the manure pile of crime, drugs, illicit sex, violence, lying, stealing, screaming, anger, false religions, and evil spiritual power. Will you reject the manure-pile choices even though you can

167

seemingly get what you want? Will you take the shortcut to "success" and hope no one finds out?

I am involved in a wonderful ministry called *Courage Worldwide* [2] that helps rescue young children who have been forced into lives of sexual slavery. The police or FBI locates the girls and bring them to a Courage House where they can unlearn the life they were forced to adopt. It is very exciting to see these young girls make new choices to redeem their life from what was forced upon them. Courage Worldwide trains hundreds of volunteers to help in stabilizing the young girls' lives. It is heartbreaking to hear what is involved in the manure pile of prostitution that these very young children were forced to adopt as normal life. It truly is a manure pile and will hold them in this life until they die from disease or beatings. Sadly, not every girl who is offered a chance to leave the life of sexual slavery chooses to stay away from that manure pile. Many are so accustomed to that life that it is the only thing they know, and they freely choose to go back to "their" manure-pile because it is what they know. In these cases, the Devil wins. It is so sad.

Belial

In 2 Corinthians 6:15, the Apostle Paul (speaking under the inspiration of the Holy Spirit) says,

> *Or what harmony has Christ with Belial, or what has a believer in common with an unbeliever?*

Here Paul gives the Devil a new title: Belial. This is a transliterated Hebrew word, Beliar or Belial. In other words,

---

[2] For more information about Courage Worldwide, visit www.courageworldwide.org.

it is the Hebrew letters b-e-l-i-a-l written in Greek letters and put in the Bible. In the Hebrew, it means baseness, worthless, wickedness, lawless. The idea behind this name is that the one given this title doesn't have moral boundaries. They make no positive contribution to society. They are parasitic on other parts of society: family, business, men, women, government, schools, etc. In fact, this person is a drain on society through their selfishness and schemes. The Devil is given this title because he has no moral stopping points. He wants to get people involved outside of moral boundaries and then convince them that they are worthless for following his lead out there.

This is really another version of the Beelzebub or manure-pile scheme. The Devil will test you with hopelessness and feelings of worthlessness. He will expose you to images, people, actions, and words that will make you feel hopeless and worthless. He wants to see if you will embrace the lie that life is not worth living, that the righteousness you can do will not make a difference. The Devil convinces many people to commit suicide by running the *Underworld-Belial Scheme* on them.

We must spend some time talking about wickedness and worthlessness. They go together in ways that many do not realize. When a person is involved in damaging others for their own person gain, they are being wicked. The act of enhancing our position, status, finances, person, or family through damage to others takes away significance and meaning. Our lives become worthless. We are just consumers with no benefit to others or the society at large. This is what the Devil wants us to feel. He wants us to engage in wicked things and then show us that others have been damaged. Then he wants to suggest that all your gain is worthless and you are worthless. It is this type of worthless behavior that typifies the Devil and Satan. People get what they want, but they leave destruction and death in their wake. Eventually the Devil will have us ruling over a vast manure pile of the remnants of getting what we selfishly wanted. At the end, the Devil floods a person with hopelessness as they sit on their manure pile surveying the way they wasted their life.

Internal and External Versions

As in each of the other schemes, there are both internal and external versions of this *Underworld Scheme*. The goal is always the same—to move you to a place where you are freely choosing to waste your life on perversions of normal life. If the Devil is running an internal version of this scheme against you, he may glamorize the underworld life through movies, books, stories, rumors, and social media. He plants the ideas in your head that this underworld life is much more exciting than the dull existence you've been experiencing. He wants you to mentally embrace a glamorized picture of some underworld existence so that you will be more susceptible to actually trying this life. I am always amazed when I hear of people who acted on the ridiculous notions of the underworld life: prostitution was glamorous; illegal drugs heightened your joy in life; occult powers would make you important; alcohol would fix your problems; crime actually paid; or molesting children would fulfill a desire. All of these perverse worlds represented by ideas and actions are manure piles. Once a person mentally embraces that these are glamorous, it is much easier to be moved toward these particular manure piles.

Another internal scheme is to dwell on hopelessness. The Devil can make almost anything appear hopeless even if it is very promising and will do a lot of good. Everyone who has attempted to do something good can testify to the time when it all felt hopeless and that nothing would come of all the efforts. Be aware of this internal scheme meant to discourage you from pursuing your dream.

If the Devil is running an external version of the *Underworld Scheme* against you, then you may experience lots of contact with a particular underworld. You may have people who are totally into a particular underworld seeking to become your friends, inviting you to their kind of fun, and/or fixing problems for you. You may be invited to a séance or a satanic ritual, or a party where there are no rules. An external *Underworld Scheme* involves real people or real spiritual rituals or wicked spirits being present in your life. When these things are present, this is not a game. You need to seek the Lord Jesus Christ and put on the whole Armor of God.

Exercises to Defeat the Underworld Scheme

How do we defeat the Devil as he uses *Underworld Scheme* on us? There are eight actions and spiritual antidotes known as the Armor of God that are essential to winning the life God has always wanted for you. They will be a crucial part of beating the temptations of the Devil. The Devil wants to destroy us and add us to his manure pile of wasted people, wasted skills, wasted opportunities, and wasted lives. But we can win the life that God has planned for us through Christ. God has given us all we need; we just have to start using all he has provided.

These spiritual weapons are truth, righteousness, peace, faith, salvation, Word of God (God's Wisdom), prayer, and alertness. The Devil acts against these qualities because in order to destroy a life, he needs to distort or attack each of these. In every scheme there is an attack against, or distortion of, one of these spiritual realities. It is these qualities that bring health, blessing, peace, and joy to people.

Let me write these again in a graphically interesting way so you will hopefully remember them. Memorize them. Use them. Write your own copy of them. Draw them. Ask God for insight on how to increase their use in your life. You and I will need these to defeat the Schemes of the Devil.

Truth

Righteousness

Peace

Faith

Salvation

Word of God

Prayer

Alertness

In these we have the answers, the antidotes, and the super-weapons that will defeat Beelzebub's *Underworld Scheme.* We also have the Holy Spirit guiding us as to which one to use at what time. Each of these spiritual weapons is a scheme buster, but we are to be guided by the Holy Spirit in our deployment of these weapons. We don't just use all the weapons every time we sense a spiritual attack; there are usually one or two that need our focus at a time. There are numerous examples in Scripture where the Holy Spirit directed people to use only one or two weapons instead of all of them (Matt. 4:1-12; Matt. 26:36-46). When I am under attack, I pray down through these spiritual weapons and ask God to guide me to just the right one for the underworld behaviors, underworld associates, and/or underworld powers I am facing.

Now it is important to note that the first three spiritual weapons are to be deployed constantly in your life. As the Apostle Paul outlines, these spiritual weapons are distinct between the first three and the last five.

Stand firm therefore, <u>HAVING</u> GIRDED YOUR LOINS WITH TRUTH, and <u>HAVING</u> PUT ON THE BREASTPLATE OF RIGHTEOUSNESS, and <u>having</u> shod YOUR FEET WITH THE PREPARATION OF THE GOSPEL OF PEACE; in addition to all, taking up the shield of faith with which you will be able to extinguish all the flaming arrows of the evil one. And take THE HELMET OF SALVATION, and the sword of the Spirit, which is the word of God. With all prayer and petition pray at all times in the Spirit, and with this in view, be on the alert with all perseverance and petition for all the saints. (Eph. 6:14-18).

Notice that for the first three, he uses the past tense verb *of having*, as in already in the past having put on these weapons: Truth, Righteousness, and Peace. You are always to be standing on truth and learning more. We are always to be righteous and loving. We are always to be peaceable and forgiving. The last five weapons are to be taken up and deployed when the battle rages: Faith, Salvation, Word of God, Prayer, and Alertness.

Engaging God in Your Spiritual Battle with Underworld people, Underworld behaviors and Underworld powers

Just as Jesus was completely dependent upon the Father and the Spirit, we are dependent upon the whole of the Trinity for our victory in the spiritual battles of our life. Too many Christians act like they are on their own when facing the Devil. They think God threw the manual (Bible) at them and told them, "Read it; all the answers are in there." God is with us and has prepared all the weapons, knows the right strategy, and will give us wisdom and guidance if we ask for it and expect to receive it. Seriously ask God the following questions when you think the Devil is tempting, testing, or scheming against you.

What spiritual weapon should I to use against this *Underworld Scheme?*

- Is it truth?
- Is it righteousness?
- Is it peace?
- Is it faith or God-ordained risk?
- Is it a God-provided way of escape or element of hope?
- Is it wisdom from God's Word?
- Is it prayer?
- Is it alertness and precaution?

Once you have answered these questions, then it is time to go deeper on the particular weapons you are supposed to deploy. In the exercises that follow I have made a lot of educated guesses about what you may need to defeat a particular scheme, but it is more important that you stay sensitive to the Lord Jesus as he guides you to the particular way of using the Armor of God to defeat the schemes of Satan. It is also very helpful to have a pastor, mentor, life coach, wise friend, or counselor help you understand how to defeat the enemy. When you are facing repeated temptations from others to participate in underworld activities internally, ask these questions and act to protect yourself. Beelzebub's underworld behaviors, underworld associates, and/or underworld powers are real. God loves us and wants us to get through this test and be stronger on the other side. If it sounds too good to be true, it probably is. If everybody else is saying that this group or theory is wrong, then it has a chance of being wrong. The Devil is always leading away from the abundant life God has planned. Don't fall for it.

Further Questions to Ask

Pray down through these questions and let God the Holy Spirit guide you to the particular spiritual weapon that he wants you to deploy against these underworld behaviors, underworld associates, and/or underworld powers you are facing.

What **truth(s)** would stop these **underworld behaviors, underworld associates, and/or underworld powers** and deliver the individual, group, or nation?

- It may be truths about God that will win the day.
- It may be truths about Christian living that will win the day.

175

- It may be truths about ourselves that will win the day.
- It may be truths about others and/or society that will win the day.
- It may be a particular scientific fact or historical field that will dispel the deception and schemes of the enemy.

What **righteousness, love, or morality** would stop these **underworld behaviors, underworld associates, and/or underworld powers** and deliver the individual, group, or nation?

- It may be that you need to increase your love in one of the relationships of your life.
- It may be that you need to increase the wisdom of the love in one of your relationships.
- It may be that you need to do good and right things that you have not been doing.
- It may be that you need to stop doing some unloving, unrighteous, or damaging actions or words.
- It may be that you need to ask about an opportunity you are being given:
  - Will this actually do good? Will this harm others?

  - Is this really just about my desire and I am being led along by my desire?

What **peace moves** or strategies would stop these **underworld behaviors, underworld associates, and/or underworld powers** and deliver the individual, group, or nation?
- It may be that you need to make peace with God in ways that you haven't yet.

- It may be that you need to examine or lower your expectations or the anger will still win.
- It may be that you need to change some of your actions or the circumstances that surround the tense moments in your life.
- It may be that you need to forgive God, yourself, or others to defeat this scheme.
- It may be that you need to turn this enemy into a friend.
- It may be that you need to stop acting with hostility in a particular situation.
- It may be that you need to start positive steps to bring about peace with others.
- It may be that you need to leave all justice with God.
- It may be that you need more than just peace you need harmony with another person.

What **faith steps** or God-directed risks would stop these **underworld behaviors, underworld associates, and/or underworld powers** and deliver the individual, group, or nation?

- It may be that you need to trust God for something that is right but very hard to do.
- It may be that you need to learn more about God and the Christian life so that your trust is more solid and informed.
- It may be that God wants you to trust him and head in a new direction to defeat this particular scheme of the Devil.
- It may be that you need to decide to trust God when it doesn't feel like the best solution.

- It may be that you must trust God when you are making no progress as that is better than the progress toward the wrong goals.

What **ways of escape (salvation) or hope** would stop these **underworld behaviors, underworld associates, and/or underworld powers** and deliver the individual, group, or nation?

- It may be that you need to explore and take fuller advantage of the salvation that is in the Lord Jesus Christ than you have in the past.
- It may be that you are supposed to take some way of escape that will get you out of a situation that is too tempting, too pressurized, too dangerous, or too life altering for you.
- It may be that you must hold on to or look for the elements of hope from your past and in the present as you wait for God's deliverance.
- It may be that you have to cling to the hope of your salvation: the return of Christ and your place in heaven to say *no* to the temptations of the Devil in this life.

What **wisdom from God's Word** would stop these **underworld behaviors, underworld associates, and/or underworld powers** and deliver the individual, group, or nation?

- It may be that you need to read the Scriptures daily so that God can prompt you with the appropriate verses when you need them.

- It may be that you need to read through the Scriptures so that you have a grasp of what God is saying in the whole of the Word of God.
- It may be that you need to go to a class, seminar, or small group where you can get a better overview of the Old and New Testament.
- It may be that you need to learn how to study the Scriptures so that when God prompts you with a verse, you can study it and gain the appropriate understanding of what God is saying.
- It may be that you need to learn how to meditate on the Word of God so that when God gives you a Scripture, you know how to carry it around in your mind all day.
- It may be that you need to quote a verse of Scripture to yourself all day to defeat the scheme the Devil is running.
- It may be that you need to quote a particular verse of Scripture at the Devil to let him know that you are on to his scheme. You now know the wisdom of God and will not be fooled by his ideas and opportunities.

What **kind and type of prayers** would stop these **underworld behaviors, underworld associates, and/or underworld powers** and deliver the individual, group, or nation?

- It may be that God prompts you to spend time praising Him as the antidote to a particular scheme of the Devil.
- It may be that God wants you to prayerfully contemplate a Scripture as the way to win against a particular scheme.
- It may be that God wants you to request certain things from him that you will need to win against this particular scheme.

- It may be that God wants you to pray for someone else to defeat this scheme.
- It may be that you need to pray prayers of gratefulness in order to pass the test that is being thrown at you.
- It may be that you need to confess your sins or the sins of the group or your nation in order to stop this scheme from succeeding.
- It may be that God wants you to battle for the unconverted soul(s) you know that need the Lord in order to defeat this particular scheme of the Devil.
- It may be that you need to pray for government officials that they would be safe and ethical as they make decisions and unthreatened by interests groups that are evil.

What **precautions and/or alertness** would stop these **underworld behaviors, underworld associates, and/or underworld powers** and deliver the individual, group, or nation?

- It may be that God wants you to make very specific preparations to withstand a scheme or test of the Devil.
- It may be that you have an exposed weakness to sin that will damage, dishonor, or destroy you if it is not dealt with; and you must protect yourself and your loved ones in some way before the storm of the test arrives.
- It may be that you do not know enough about a crucial relationship or truth of Christianity and God is giving you the heads-up about learning how to make that right. You must act before the test comes, or it will hurt you or stop your progress.

Scheme #8

The God of This World Scheme

(Amplified Importance)

His name was Rusty. He was a very good mechanic and people flocked to have him work on their cars. He always did good work and could solve problems that stumped other mechanics. But Rusty began to read his own press clippings. He had heard so many people praise his car repair skills that he started arguing with the other mechanics and his bosses. Since he was clearly the best mechanic in the garage, he wanted to be paid more. He kept demanding to be listened to and compensated at twice what the other mechanics were getting. Eventually his arguing and complaining about hours, pay, and respect were too much; and he was let go even though he brought lots of customers into the shop. I met Rusty when he was unemployed, waiting to be hired by another garage. I knew him for five years as he grappled with his skills and the fact that no one would pay him what he thought he was worth or give him the respect that he knew he deserved. He made statements like, "Nobody complains when you pay your doctor a lot of money to keep your body running. I am the doctor of people's cars, but they won't pay me what my skills are worth!" "I refuse to be treated like a peon when I clearly know more about cars than the manager of the garage." Rusty had fallen for *The God of This World Scheme*. He had an inflated sense of his own importance and allowed himself to be puffed up by the praise that others were giving him. He was a god of auto repair and he would be treated like it, or he wouldn't work at all.

Rusty took his wife and family through years of silly schemes, ill-advised moves, public assistance, and significant depravation all because he would not humble himself and use his considerable skills within the boundaries of reasonable pay and authority guidelines. He insisted that he be treated with an outsized respect because of what he knew and could do with cars. He really wanted to be treated as a god because of his knowledge and skills with cars. His incredible arrogance about his place in the world kept destroying his life and his family's life. There are thousands of "Rustys" in all walks of life who have fallen for an amplified sense of their own importance. When we look at them we can see that they are making way too much of themselves, and it will cost them. They are robbing themselves of God's abundant life while they proclaim loudly that they are experts, authorities, and gurus about some subject. They believe that they are gods of the particular world they chose to inhabit.

The Devil delights to take your skills in one area and puff them up so that you feel a level of importance beyond the real importance of your abilities. We see this with teenage football and basketball players who are given everything they want because they can run fast or shoot well. They begin to believe that they are gods of their world. They should have everything they want. They should have people constantly telling them how important they are. This scheme amplifies a person's sense of importance and then always removes the importance later and crushes the person. We would all like to believe that we are more important than our skills, abilities, or gifts, but if we allow ourselves to go down that road we will be falling for a scheme of Satan. Just because you closed an important deal for your company doesn't mean you can be immoral, unethical, racist or violent. Your accomplishment doesn't make you a god, but the Devil wants you believe it does. The rules don't apply to you anymore.

This scheme is what the Devil runs against athletes who are especially gifted. Because they can run fast, jump high, throw a pass, or shoot a ball, they should get special treatment; they are gods, and so the normal rules of life don't apply to them. This special treatment keeps going until they are injured or too old and then they are pushed aside for the next god. The number of young men and women who have fallen for this scheme is in the thousands.

This is also what happens to stars in the music industry and Hollywood. These two industries promote the idea that if you have acting skills or musical skills and they can make money off of your talent, then the normal rules of morality don't apply. You are a god and can do whatever you want in the rest of your life as long as you keep making money for the industry big-wigs. Too many young performers have been puffed up to believe that they are mini gods and then their fifteen minutes of fame are over, and they are cast aside and out of work. But then you are stuck with the lie of believing you are a god, and you must live with all you have done when you were living this life style. This is the lie of *The God of This World Scheme.*

I have watched this scheme capture men and women from every economic class and every culture. The Devil helps amplify people's own importance to where they are gods in their own mind in charge of their own domain. One very savvy pastor at the Los Angeles rescue mission told me that this amplified sense of importance is the root cause of many of the people who were at the mission. They refused to listen to their spouse, they refused to listen to a boss, and they don't want anyone to tell them what to do. They were the kings of their lives and if they wanted to drink or do whatever, then that was what they were going to do. They would rather be on skid row than have anybody tell them what to do. They are the gods of their life. They were not wrong; everyone else was wrong. Interestingly, many of the people who are at the rescue missions or shelters move out of that life when they are willing to accept help, training, and practice new habits.

Explanation of *The God of This World Scheme*

The Devil thinks of himself and has become in some sense the god of this world -- a puny planet he rules (2 Cor. 4:4; Luke 4:5-7; John 12:31; 16:11). It doesn't mean that he really is God or that he doesn't have to pass his ideas through the real God Almighty, but the Devil deceives himself because of the assignments that God has given him. We all are tempted to want to rule our little worlds, and we can be tricked into giving up true riches to rule over a very small little world, such as our marriage, a person, a company, a country, etc. You want the complete power over this little area, and you sell your soul to get it. You cheat, lie, steal, pervert, and oppress just to have this control or sense of importance. It is always small compared with the blessings of God and an integrated approach to living. You are in authority and under authority and have far more influence that way. This is why we hear of men beating or imprisoning their wives. This is why pimps enslave the girls they pull into their little ring of evil. This is why some bosses are complete jerks, always needing to exert their control and power.

The Devil is constantly whispering to people that they can be the god of their world by just a little more power, just a little more illicit activity, just a little more anger, just a little more lying. He loves when people embrace his lies and give into a sense of amplified importance. If he can get you to believe that you are more important than you really are, then he can suggest ways to act to enhance your importance and actions that you deserve because you are that important.

Verses

Since this is an unusual title for the Devil it can trip people up, so lets look at a number of places in Scripture where God gives the Devil this title and a number of places where we see the Devil run this scheme against Biblical characters.

2 Corinthians 4:4 - *in whose case **the god of this world** has blinded the minds of the unbelieving so that they might not see the light of the gospel of the glory of Christ, who is the image of God.*

In this verse the Apostle Paul tells us that the Devil has become god to people who have completely oriented their lives to his ideas, his goals, and his means. The Devil does rule over these people and in ruling over them he (the Devil) makes sure that they stay blinded to the wonder of the gospel. As we have already seen, the Devil is self-deceived about his real power and authority but he does rule over the people who fall for his schemes and wicked seductions. There will come a day when the Devil and all his demons are cast into the lake of fire (Rev 20:10), and the delusion of their rulership over this world will finally be put to rest.

The Devil tried to tempt Christ with this *God of this World Scheme*:

> *And he led Him up and showed Him all the kingdoms of the world in a moment of time. And the Devil said to Him, "I will give You all this*

185

domain and its glory; for it has been handed over to me, and I give it to whomever I wish. Therefore if You worship before me, it shall all be Yours. " Luke 4:5-7

Notice that this is the ultimate *God of this World Scheme.* The Devil is the "god" of this planet in as much as the true Almighty God has put him in charge of the testing and evil dimensions of human interaction on this planet. The Devil has an inflated idea of how important he really is and offers all of this inflated importance to Jesus if He will just worship him.

Jesus is aware of the fact that all power and authority will ultimately be given to Him again after He accomplishes the mission of becoming Savior of the world, so He rejects this reduced offer of amplified importance. Also notice that the Devil's offer of god of this world to Jesus is a head fake because it starts with accepting the Devil's authority over Him. This is always how The God of This World Scheme works. It promises you an amplified sense of importance in some area or control over a certain part of life, but there is always another authority (usually demonic and/or evil) over the top of you.

Jesus rejects this scheme just as we should. When we follow God's direction and plan, we gain far more authority than we ever would by becoming belligerent, arrogant, violent, or evil.

The next two verses deal with the same idea (god of this world) but use slightly different wording in the title given to Satan. In these verses he is called the ruler of this world.

John 12:31 - *Now judgment is upon this world; now the ruler of this world will be cast out.*

John 16:11 - *and concerning judgment, because the ruler of this world has been judged.*

Satan is called the ruler of this world in that he has been given significant latitude to deceive and tempt mankind to follow him. He acts as a ruler over those who follow him, keeping them deceived and feeding on sin. The scheme that he runs on others is the one he has deluded himself into believing: that he actually is a god over these people and gains importance in his own eyes because of who follows him. It is this feeling of importance that is the goal. Satan still has to submit his plans for temptation and testing to God before he can act (Job 1), but he tries to ignore those moments of submission and focus on his power over those who follow him.

He tries to get men and women to also fall for this same self-delusion and believe that they are the gods of their own worlds with power, importance, and control over others. If he can get you to believe that you are so important that normal rules and moral boundaries no longer apply to you then you will do wicked things to maintain your control. He can also keep you satisfied with your feeling of importance rather than doing some good work that you are supposed to do.

It is important to note -- as is stated in the verses above -- that because of Jesus Christ's work on the cross, the Devil has been judged. Jesus the Christ has paid for the sins of mankind and released us from any rulership the Devil may have claimed over us. We are free to pursue God and the maximum life that He has planned for us. We no longer have to live under the Devil's over-lordship, and we do not have to fall for our own *God of this World Scheme* just to sneak some level of meaning and significance into the world. We are a part of a grand plan of redemption in Christ. God has searched through time and all the cultures of the world to offer you and I the opportunity to respond to love of God. Don't miss this. Respond to God's love and keep responding and you will build an unbelievable life as the servant of the Most High.

Notice that in these verses the Devil offers this same *God of this World Scheme* to Adam and Eve and they fall for it completely. They become convinced by the Devil that God Almighty is holding things back from them. If they only were to reach out and take the fruit of the knowledge of good and evil they would become their own gods. He essentially is saying that they could rule the garden as gods themselves and not have to submit to God Almighty at all. They could know far more than they know now. Look at the text of Genesis 3:1-7:

> *Now the serpent was more crafty than any beast of the field which the LORD God had made. And he said to the woman, "Indeed, has God said, 'You shall not eat from any tree of the garden'?" The woman said to the serpent, "From the fruit of the trees of the garden we may eat; but from the fruit of the tree which is in the middle of the garden, God has said, 'You shall not eat from it or touch it, or you will die.'" The serpent said to the woman, "You surely will not die! For God knows that in the day you eat from it your eyes will be opened, <u>and you will be like God</u>, knowing good and evil." When the woman saw that the tree was good for food, and that it was a delight to the eyes, and that the tree was desirable to make one wise, she took from its fruit and ate; and she gave also to her*

husband with her, and he ate. Then the eyes of both of them were opened, and they knew that they were naked; and they sewed fig leaves together and made themselves loin coverings.

Unfortunately Adam and Eve fell right into the trap of the Devil. We all want more than we have, and the Devil uses that to pull on our discontentment until we jump into some huge mistake because we want to be our own god. Adam and Eve's decision to pursue their own godhood cut them and us off from our connection to the Lord God Almighty. The same thing is true of us when we fall for the Devil's temptations to be our own god instead of constantly recognizing and exalting the deity of God the Father, God the Son, and God the Holy Spirit. There is greater authority under the authority of God than grasping for importance and control outside of His plan.

In these verses, we read of how the angel Lucifer originally introduced sin into this good universe by falling for this God of this World Scheme. The angel Lucifer was given a hugely exalted position as anointed cherub who covers. Even though this was the most exalted angelic position, it required a certain level of submissiveness to the Lord God Almighty. Lucifer decided that he should have more importance and more control and it led him to sin in his heart and through his actions. God traces Lucifer's thoughts as he fell for this God of this World Scheme.

How you have fallen from heaven, O star of the morning, son of the dawn! You have been cut down to the earth, You who have weakened the nations! But you said in your heart, "I will ascend to heaven; I will raise my throne above the stars of God, And I will sit on the mount of assembly In the recesses of the north. I will ascend above the heights

of the clouds; I will make myself like the Most
High." Nevertheless you will be thrust down to
Sheol, To the recesses of the pit. Isaiah 14:12-14

Notice that God must judge this grab for authority, power, and importance beyond what God had planned into the universe. When you grasp for authority that has not been offered by a legitimate leader, then it will result in your demotion and your plans being crushed. Even what you do have will be taken away.

One of the classic examples of The God of This World Scheme is what happened to Nebuchadnezzar in Daniel 4. The King of Babylon -- during this period -- Nebuchadnezzar, had conquered the known world and saw himself as the god of the whole world. God tried to break the power of The God of This World Scheme in Nebuchadnezzar's life before judgment fell, but it did no good and the king had to go through the insanity that comes from full embrace of this scheme. After Nebuchadnezzar had been restored to sanity, he penned these words to tell us what he went through because of falling for this *God of this World Scheme.*

Nebuchadnezzar the king to all the peoples, nations,
and men of every language that live in all the earth:
May your peace abound! It has seemed good to me
to declare the signs and wonders which the Most
High God has done for me. How great are His signs
And how mighty are His wonders! His kingdom is
an everlasting kingdom And His dominion is from
generation to generation. I, Nebuchadnezzar, was
at ease in my house and flourishing in my palace. I
saw a dream and it made me fearful; and these
fantasies as I lay on my bed and the visions in my
mind kept alarming me. So I gave orders to bring
into my presence all the wise men of Babylon that

they might make known to me the interpretation of the dream. Then the magicians, the conjurers, the Chaldeans and the diviners came in and I related the dream to them, but they could not make its interpretation known to me. But finally Daniel came in before me, whose name is Belteshazzar according to the name of my god, and in whom is a spirit of the holy gods; and I related the dream to him, saying, O Belteshazzar, chief of the magicians, since I know that a spirit of the holy gods is in you and no mystery baffles you, tell me the visions of my dream which I have seen, along with its interpretation. Now these were the visions in my mind as I lay on my bed: I was looking, and behold, there was a tree in the midst of the earth and its height was great. The tree grew large and became strong And its height reached to the sky, And it was visible to the end of the whole earth. Its foliage was beautiful and its fruit abundant, And in it was food for all. The beasts of the field found shade under it, And the birds of the sky dwelt in its branches, And all living creatures fed themselves from it. I was looking in the visions in my mind as I lay on my bed, and behold, an angelic watcher, a holy one, descended from heaven. He shouted out and spoke as follows: Chop down the tree and cut off its branches, Strip off its foliage and scatter its fruit; Let the beasts flee from under it And the birds from its branches. Yet leave the stump with its roots in the ground, But with a band of iron and bronze around it, In the new grass of the field; And let him be drenched with the dew of heaven, And let him share with the beasts in the grass of the earth. Let his mind be changed from that of a man And let a beast's mind be given to him, And let seven periods of time pass over him. This sentence is by the decree of the angelic watchers And the decision is a command of the holy ones, In order that the living may know That the Most High is ruler over the realm of mankind, And bestows it on whom He wishes And sets over it the lowliest of men. This is the dream which I, King Nebuchadnezzar, have seen. Now you, Belteshazzar, tell me its interpretation, inasmuch as none of the wise men of my kingdom is able to make known to me the interpretation; but you are able, for a spirit of the holy gods is in you. Then Daniel, whose name is Belteshazzar, was appalled for a while as his thoughts alarmed him. The king responded and said, Belteshazzar, do not let the dream or its interpretation alarm you. Belteshazzar replied, My lord, if only the dream applied to those who hate you and its interpretation to your adversaries! The tree that you saw, which became large and grew strong, whose height reached to the sky and was visible to all the earth and whose foliage was beautiful and its fruit abundant, and in which was food for all, under which the beasts of the field dwelt and in whose branches the birds of the sky lodged -- it is you, O king; for you have become great and grown strong, and your majesty has become great and reached to the sky and your dominion to the end of the earth. In that the king saw an angelic watcher, a holy one, descending from heaven and saying, Chop down the tree and destroy it; yet leave the stump with its roots in the ground, but with a band of iron and bronze around it in the new grass of the field, and let him be drenched with the dew of heaven, and let him share with the beasts of the field until seven periods of time pass over him, this is the interpretation, O king, and this is the decree of the Most High, which has come upon my lord the king: that you be driven away from mankind and your dwelling place be with the beasts of the field, and you be given grass to eat like cattle and be drenched with the dew of heaven; and seven periods of time will pass over you, until you recognize that the Most High is ruler over the realm of mankind and bestows it on whomever He wishes. And in that it was commanded to leave the stump with the roots of the tree, your kingdom will be assured to you after you recognize that it is Heaven that rules. Therefore, O king, may my advice be pleasing to you: break away now from your sins by doing righteousness and from your iniquities by showing mercy to the poor, in case there may be a prolonging of your prosperity. All this happened to Nebuchadnezzar the king. "Twelve months later he was walking on the roof of the royal palace of Babylon. The king reflected and said, Is this not Babylon the great, which I myself have built as a royal residence by the might of my power and for the glory of my majesty? While the word was in the king's mouth, a voice came from heaven, saying, King Nebuchadnezzar, to you it is declared: sovereignty has been removed from you, and you will be driven away from mankind, and your dwelling place will be with the beasts of the field. You will be given grass to eat like cattle, and seven periods of time will pass over you until you recognize that the Most High is ruler over the realm of mankind and bestows it on whomever He wishes.

*Immediately the word concerning Nebuchadnezzar
was fulfilled; and he was driven away from
mankind and began eating grass like cattle, and his
body was drenched with the dew of heaven until his
hair had grown like eagles' feathers and his nails
like birds' claws. But at the end of that period, I,
Nebuchadnezzar, raised my eyes toward heaven
and my reason returned to me, and I blessed the
Most High and praised and honored Him who lives
forever; For His dominion is an everlasting
dominion, And His kingdom endures from
generation to generation. All the inhabitants of the
earth are accounted as nothing, But He does
according to His will in the host of heaven And
among the inhabitants of earth; And no one can
ward off His hand Or say to Him, What have You
done? At that time my reason returned to me. And
my majesty and splendor were restored to me for the
glory of my kingdom, and my counselors and my
nobles began seeking me out; so I was reestablished
in my sovereignty, and surpassing greatness was
added to me. Now I, Nebuchadnezzar, praise, exalt
and honor the King of heaven, for all His works are
true and His ways just, and He is able to humble
those who walk in pride.*

Internal and External Versions

The point of this *God of this World Scheme* is for the person
to embrace an amplified view of their own importance to the
point where they do and say things that lead them to sin
against God Almighty and others in their world. The internal
versions of this scheme are thoughts and feelings that take us

past a sense of significance and meaning and move us to arrogance, oppression, bigotry, haughtiness, and the like.

An external version of this *God of this World Scheme* is when others come around you and puff you up with your importance and make you feel that you deserve to act immorally or unethically. It is amazing that you can always find these kinds of people who will magnify your importance so you will sin in the ways that they are already sinning. There are whole sections of American culture that seem to be built on the idea of convincing people to throw out morality because they have already done it. They want you to be verbally abusive; they want you to be mentally abusive; they want you to abuse your employees or employers; they want you to be rebellious of all authority; they want you to be violent, sexually abusive, and sexually experimental. They want you to steal, to lie, and to scheme against people you know. All of these ideas sound reasonable to them because they have become their own god, and they want you to join them in living a horrible life of grasping and devaluing everyone and everything because you are so valuable.

Exercises to Defeat The God of This World Scheme

How do we defeat the Devil as he uses *The God of This World Scheme* on us? There are eight actions and spiritual antidotes known as the Armor of God that are essential to winning the life God has always wanted for you. They will be a crucial part of beating the temptations of the Devil. The Devil wants to destroy us and add us to the people who have such an inflated idea of themselves that they are no good to anyone. But we can win the life that God has planned for us through Christ. God has given us all we need; we just have to start using all He has provided.

These spiritual weapons are truth, righteousness, peace, faith, salvation, Word of God (God's Wisdom), prayer, and alertness. The Devil acts against these qualities because in order to destroy a life, he needs to distort or attack each of these. In every scheme there is an attack against, or distortion of, one of these spiritual realities. It is these qualities that bring health, blessing, peace, and joy to people.

Let me write these again in a graphically interesting way so you will hopefully remember them. Memorize them. Use them. Write your own copy of them. Draw them. Ask God for insight on how to increase their use in your life. You and I will need these to defeat the Schemes of the Devil.

Truth

Righteousness

Peace

Faith

Salvation

Word of God

Prayer

Alertness

In these we have the answers, the antidotes, and the super-weapons that will defeat *The God of This World Scheme*. We also have the Holy Spirit guiding us as to which one to use at what time. Each of these spiritual weapons is a scheme buster, but we are to be guided by the Holy Spirit in our deployment of these weapons. We don't just use all the weapons every time we sense a spiritual attack; there are usually one or two that need our focus at a time. There are numerous examples in Scripture where the Holy Spirit directed people to use only one or two weapons instead of all of them (Matt. 4:1-12; Matt. 26:36-46). When I am under attack, I pray down through these spiritual weapons and ask God to guide me to just the right one for the underworld behaviors, underworld associates, and/or underworld powers I am facing.

Now it is important to note that the first three spiritual weapons are to be deployed constantly in your life. As the Apostle Paul outlines, these spiritual weapons are distinct between the first three and the last five.

> *Stand firm therefore, <u>HAVING</u> GIRDED YOUR LOINS WITH TRUTH, and <u>HAVING</u> PUT ON THE BREASTPLATE OF RIGHTEOUSNESS, and having shod YOUR FEET WITH THE PREPARATION OF THE GOSPEL OF PEACE; in addition to all, taking up the shield of faith with which you will be able to extinguish all the flaming arrows of the evil one. And take THE HELMET OF SALVATION, and the sword of the Spirit, which is the word of God. With all prayer and petition pray at all times in the Spirit, and with this in view, be on the alert with all perseverance and petition for all the saints, (Eph. 6:14-18).*

Notice that for the first three, he uses the past tense verb *of having*, as in already in the past having put on these weapons: Truth, Righteousness, and Peace. You are always to be standing on truth and learning more. We are always to be righteous and loving. We are always to be peaceable and forgiving. The last five weapons are to be taken up and

197

deployed when the battle rages: Faith, Salvation, Word of God, Prayer, and Alertness.

Engaging God in Your Spiritual Battle with The God of this World

Just as Jesus was completely dependent upon the Father and the Spirit, we are dependent upon the whole of the Trinity for our victory in the spiritual battles of our life. Too many Christians act like they are on their own when facing the Devil. They think God threw the manual (Bible) at them and told them, "Read it; all the answers are in there." God is with us and has prepared all the weapons, knows the right strategy, and will give us wisdom and guidance if we ask for it and expect to receive it. Seriously ask God the following questions when you think the Devil is tempting, testing, or scheming against you.

What spiritual weapon should I to use against this *God of this World Scheme?*

- Is it truth?
- Is it righteousness?
- Is it peace?
- Is it faith or God-ordained risk?
- Is it a God-provided way of escape or element of hope?
- Is it wisdom from God's Word?
- Is it prayer?
- Is it alertness and precaution?

Once you have answered these questions, then it is time to go deeper on the particular weapons you are supposed to deploy. In the exercises that follow I have made a lot of educated guesses about what you may need to defeat a particular scheme, but it is more important that you stay sensitive to the Lord Jesus as he guides you to the particular

198

way of using the Armor of God to defeat the schemes of Satan. It is also very helpful to have a pastor, mentor, life coach, wise friend, or counselor help you understand how to defeat the enemy. When you are facing repeated temptations from others to participate in activities that amplify your sense of importance above others, ask these questions and act to protect yourself. God loves us and wants us to get through this test and be stronger on the other side. If it sounds too good to be true, it probably is. If everybody else is saying that this group or theory is wrong, then it has a chance of being wrong. The Devil is always leading away from the abundant life God has planned. Don't fall for it.

Further Questions to Ask

Pray down through these questions and let God the Holy Spirit guide you to the particular spiritual weapon that He wants you to deploy against god of this world thoughts and activities you are facing.

What **truth(s)** would stop these **amplified feelings of importance, power, and control** and deliver the individual, group, or nation?

- It may be truths about God that will win the day.
- It may be truths about Christian living that will win the day.
- It may be truths about ourselves that will win the day.
- It may be truths about others and/or society that will win the day.
- It may be a particular scientific fact or historical field that will dispel the deception and schemes of the enemy.

What **righteousness, love, or morality** would stop these **amplified feelings of importance, power, and control** and deliver the individual, group, or nation?

- It may be that you need to increase your love in one of the relationships of your life.
- It may be that you need to increase the wisdom of the love in one of your relationships.
- It may be that you need to do good and right things that you have not been doing.
- It may be that you need to stop doing some unloving, unrighteous, or damaging actions or words.
- It may be that you need to ask about an opportunity you are being given:
  - Will this actually do good? Will this harm others?
  - Is this really just about my desire and I am being led along by my desire?

What **peace moves** or strategies would stop these **amplified feelings of importance, power, and control** and deliver the individual, group, or nation?

- It may be that you need to make peace with God in ways that you haven't yet.
- It may be that you need to examine or lower your expectations or the anger will still win.
- It may be that you need to change some of your actions or the circumstances that surround the tense moments in your life.
- It may be that you need to forgive God, yourself, or others to defeat this scheme.

- It may be that you need to turn this enemy into a friend.
- It may be that you need to stop acting with hostility in a particular situation.
- It may be that you need to start positive steps to bring about peace with others.
- It may be that you need to leave all justice with God.
- It may be that you need more than just peace you need harmony with another person.

What **faith steps** or God directed risks would stop these **amplified feelings of importance, power, and control** and deliver the individual, group, or nation?

- It may be that you need to trust God for something that is right but very hard to do.
- It may be that you need to learn more about God and the Christian life so that your trust is more solid and informed.
- It may be that God wants you to trust him and head in a new direction to defeat this particular scheme of the Devil.
- It may be that you need to decide to trust God when it doesn't feel like the best solution.
- It may be that you must trust God when you are making no progress as that is better than the progress toward the wrong goals.

What **ways of escape (salvation) or hope** would stop these **amplified feelings of importance, power, and control** and deliver the individual, group, or nation?

- It may be that you need to explore and take fuller advantage of the salvation that is in the Lord Jesus Christ than you have in the past.
- It may be that you are supposed to take some way of escape that will get you out of a situation that is too tempting, too pressurized, too dangerous, or too life altering for you.
- It may be that you must hold on to or look for the elements of hope from your past and in the present as you wait for God's deliverance.
- It may be that you have to cling to the hope of your salvation: the return of Christ and your place in heaven to say *no* to the temptations of the Devil in this life.

What **wisdom from God's Word** would stop these **amplified feelings of importance, power, and control** and deliver the individual, group, or nation?

- It may be that you need to read the Scriptures daily so that God can prompt you with the appropriate verses when you need them.
- It may be that you need to read through the Scriptures so that you have a grasp of what God is saying in the whole of the Word of God.
- It may be that you need to go to a class, seminar, or small group where you can get a better overview of the Old and New Testament.
- It may be that you need to learn how to study the Scriptures so that when God prompts you with a verse, you can study it and gain the appropriate understanding of what God is saying.

- It may be that you need to learn how to meditate on the Word of God so that when God gives you a Scripture, you know how to carry it around in your mind all day.
- It may be that you need to quote a verse of Scripture to yourself all day to defeat the scheme the Devil is running.
- It may be that you need to quote a particular verse of Scripture at the Devil to let him know that you are on to his scheme. You now know the wisdom of God and will not be fooled by his ideas and opportunities.

What **kind and type of prayers** would stop these **amplified feelings of importance, power, and control** and deliver the individual, group, or nation?

- It may be that God prompts you to spend time praising Him as the antidote to a particular scheme of the Devil.
- It may be that God wants you to prayerfully contemplate a Scripture as the way to win against a particular scheme.
- It may be that God wants you to request certain things from him that you will need to win against this particular scheme.
- It may be that God wants you to pray for someone else to defeat this scheme.
- It may be that you need to pray prayers of gratefulness in order to pass the test that is being thrown at you.
- It may be that you need to confess your sins or the sins of the group or your nation in order to stop this scheme from succeeding.
- It may be that God wants you to battle for the unconverted soul(s) you know that need the Lord in order to defeat this particular scheme of the Devil.

- It may be that you need to pray for government officials that they would be safe and ethical as they make decisions and unthreatened by interests groups that are evil.

What **precautions and/or alertness** would stop these **amplified feelings of importance, power, and control** and deliver the individual, group, or nation?

- It may be that God wants you to make very specific preparations to withstand a scheme or test of the Devil.
- It may be that you have an exposed weakness to sin that will damage, dishonor, or destroy you if it is not dealt with; and you must protect yourself and your loved ones in some way before the storm of the test arrives.
- It may be that you do not know enough about a crucial relationship or truth of Christianity and God is giving you the heads-up about learning how to make that right. You must act before the test comes, or it will hurt you or stop your progress.

Conclusion

The Schemes of Satan

In 57 A.D., the Apostle Paul sent a second letter to a small group of Christians who lived in one of the most wicked and debauched cities in the world: Corinth. He tells them that they must forgive a man who had taken advantage of their fellowship. The man had seized upon the grace of God as a license for giving vent to his desire to have a sexual relationship with his stepmother. His brazen sinfulness was beyond what was taboo in a place like Corinth. His sin gave the church a reputation of promoting gross immorality under the all-forgiving nature of God's grace in Christ. This type of sin had to be stopped. The church leaders expelled the man from the fellowship and called upon him to repent of his ways. Even the Apostle Paul had handed the man over to Satan to be punished for his immorality. Under the conviction of the Spirit, the consequences of his sin, the torments of the Devil, and the exclusion from the community of believers, the man repented and abandoned his sin. In the second letter to the church, Paul noted that since the man had repented, the church must forgive him or the church will be falling for one of the Schemes of the Devil—*the Satan Scheme*. The man had previously fallen for the *Tempter's Amplified Desire Scheme,* and now the church was being tempted to become a part of the *Satan Scheme* through constant accusation after true confession and repentance. It is to this small group of house churches that God speaks clearly about their knowledge of the schemes of the Satan. You know what he will try and do to you. Don't fall for his strategies.

The modern church needs to know the schemes of Satan, which is why I have written this book. You now know the seven basic schemes Satan uses and how to use the Armor of God to thwart what he is trying to do. Do not fall victim to the same basic corrupted plays he has been running for over four thousand years. Like a good football player, recognize the strategy of the opponent and resist what the Devil is trying to do. Resist him through truth, righteousness, peace, faith, salvation, the Word of God, prayer, and alertness.

Let's review what we have seen in this book.

Titles and Names for Satan

Remember, there are over nineteen different titles and names given to the angelic being, Lucifer, who corrupted himself and became what we know of as the Devil and Satan. Each one of these names and titles describes a way he tests, tempts, and tries humanity—they describe his schemes.

- Lucifer - Isaiah 14:12; Ezekiel 28:12-19
- Beelzebub - Matthew 12:24
- Satan - Job 1
- The Devil - 1 Peter 5:8
- Roaring Lion - 1 Peter 5:8
- Belial - 2 Corinthians 6:15
- Deceiver - Revelation 12:9
- Father of Lies - John 8:44
- Murderer - John 8:44
- Sinner - 1 John 3:8
- Enemy - Matthew 13:39
- Evil One - Matthew 13:39

- Angel of Light - 2 Corinthians 11:13
- God of the World - 2 Corinthians 4:4
- The Dragon - Revelation 13
- The Snake - Genesis 3
- Prince of the Power of the Air - Ephesians 2
- Ruler of this World - John 17, 1 John 5:19
- The Wicked One - Matthew 13:19; Ephesians 6:16

Types of Schemes

I have grouped the above various titles into eight basic categories so that it is easier to perceive the scheme Satan is running. I have put the modern day title and the biblical title(s) in brackets next to the scheme. Each one of these schemes is designed to get us off track to miss God's best. Satan wants us to waste our lives on something other than what God had planned for us (Eph. 2:10). He does not really care which scheme you fall for, just that you do not fulfill God's purpose for your life or Christ's abundant life for you (John 10:10). These larger satanic themes help us more quickly understand the angle that the Devil is taking against us. We have looked in depth at these seven dominant Schemes of Satan. These elements are what to look for in your life. When these markers are happening to us or around us, then the Devil is at work. He is testing you, hoping that you will fail which will allow him more ways to attack you. Embrace the Armor of God at new levels and resist what the Devil is doing. Remember that winning means a righteous, productive, and meaningful life. God has provided in Christ Jesus all you need to win. It is important that you win, not just for you but for all the people in your life. If you surrender to the Schemes of Satan, it makes it easier for all of those around you to surrender also. Look hard at these seven schemes, and ask yourself, "Is the Devil running any of these schemes against me right now?" We have examined each of these schemes and temptations so that we are not surprised when they show up in our life.

1. **The Tempter Scheme - Amplified Desire**

2. **The Devil Scheme - Amplified Lies and Accusations**

3. **The Satan Scheme - Amplified Opposition**

4. **The Roaring Lion Scheme - Amplified Fear**

5. **The Angel of Light Scheme - Amplified Power and Wisdom**

6. **The Dragon Scheme - Amplified Anger**

7. **The Underworld (Beelzebub) Scheme - Amplified Sin**

8. **The God of This World Scheme – Amplified Importance, Control and Power**

Internal and External Versions

We have seen that each scheme manifests either internally or externally. The internal versions are where the Devil puts thoughts, choices, emotions, and attitudes into our minds and souls to see if we will embrace them as our own. It is very important to realize that not every thought we think is from our own brain. The Devil has the ability to plant a thought, a choice, an emotion, and an attitude. We can choose to reject these negative, corrupted, immoral ideas as foreign; or we can choose to embrace them and play with them, mentally allowing their toxicity to leak into our thinking, choosing, and emoting. It may be that we all of a sudden have an amplification of fear or condemnation in our life that seemingly comes out of nowhere. These are internal versions of *The Amplified Fear Scheme* (Roaring Lion) and *The*

Amplified Lies and Accusation Scheme (Devil). We could find ourselves suddenly thinking about some amplified desire or some friend who we know has connections to a perverted life. These are internal versions of *The Amplified Desire Scheme* (Tempter) and *The Underworld Scheme* (Beelzebub).

There is also an external version of each of the schemes. This is where a person, an organization, or an institution comes against us using one of the satanic schemes. Just as Peter at one time was flipped to suggest that Jesus didn't need to go to the cross and die, so any person we know could be a part of an external version of a satanic scheme. The whole of the Jewish and Roman governments was used to run *The Amplified Opposition Scheme* (Satan) against Jesus so that he would be killed. Interestingly enough, God allowed that scheme to be run in that way because it was God's predestined plan to have Jesus be killed for the sins of the whole world. Their opposition to Jesus through the work of the Devil perfectly fulfilled the work of God. Sometimes a close friend may be saying things that freak you out or a colleague at work starts spreading rumors about you. These are *The Roaring Lion* and *the Devil Schemes* being run against you. It is also possible that you might become a part of a demonic scheme against someone else if you do not follow the biblical advice to never let truth and loving-kindness leave you and to let no unwholesome word proceed from your mouth (Prov. 3:3; Eph. 4:29).

The Major Relationships of Life

At times the Devil will run these schemes directed toward one particular area or relationship in my life. When the tests, trials, and temptations come, I need to be ready to apply the Armor of God to that area and trust Christ while I am resisting what Satan wants me to do. Look at each relationship of life and see if the Devil is running a scheme against that area. It is entirely possible that he has been scheming against a particular part of your life for a long time, and you have not noticed the scheme. You've probably accepted the Devil's work against you as "normal" in that area of your life. Ask some wise people to look at your life and see if you are being deceived in a particular area. Notice if you have a lot of problems in a particular area. That might mean that you have accepted a way of living in that area even though it is really built on a lie or a faulty practice. Too many times we think the way we have been living in a particular area of our lives is normal when it really isn't the way that Christ knows it can be. It may be under the control of a particular scheme, and we need to uncover and thwart the Devil's work.

- God
- Personal Development
- Marriage
- Family
- Work
- Church
- Money
- Society
- Friends
- Enemies

Remember, the Devil's goal is to destroy your life from reaching the level it could. Too often we think the goal in life is wealth, position, status, power, or pleasure; but these can't satisfy without relationships. The Devil really does want you to waste your life through your own choices. He is perfectly comfortable allowing a society to destroy the lives of its citizens through injustice, bad laws, and poor social theory or the person themselves destroying their life through giving in to various impulses and desires. But he is also personally active in giving individuals every opportunity to destroy their life.

The point of this book is not to have you looking for the Devil, but to increase your ability to embrace the wonderful life that Jesus Christ came to give you. I am so encouraged that you have stayed with us through this whole course. Remember, Jesus Christ has given us all that we need to live a victorious Christian life. Do not live in fear of the Devil but, instead, live in the fear of the Lord. The more we walk in the light, the more freedom and joy we experience. Yes, we all have areas of our life that are not completely as Christ would want them to be, but we can rejoice in how far we have already come in our spiritual journey with Christ. There will always be more to know, more to do, and more to enjoy. Pray this little prayer of dedication to the Lord Jesus Christ

Dear Lord Jesus,

I love you and I want to live the life you have planned for me before the world began. I admit that I am a sinner and have followed the Devil's schemes in the past. I ask that you would empower me to see when he is tricking me to abandon the righteous path through excessive desire, accusations, opposition, fear, spiritual power or wisdom, amplified anger, and/or the underworld. Right now, I resist the work of the Devil through the power and blood of the Lord Jesus Christ. I may at times in the future be tricked into the Devil's way for a time, but I pray for grace and thank you for the fact that there is no condemnation for those who are in Christ Jesus. Thank you that the Devil is a defeated foe; and I can find all the grace, mercy, and joy I need in Jesus Christ.

In the Name of the Lord Jesus Christ,
Amen

The Armor of God

The Armor of God is the key to resisting and thwarting the testing, temptations, trials, and attacks of the Devil. Throughout the Scriptures we see the spiritual giants of the faith resisting and winning against the Devil through the use of these basic spiritual weapons. Jesus used the *Word of God* when he faced the Devil in his temptation in the wilderness (Matthew 4). Job used *righteousness* to build a hedge of protection around himself and his family (Job 1). Peter used *truth* to thwart Ananias and Sapphira's demonically induced attack on the church (Acts 5). Ananias used *faith* to follow God's instruction and led Saul into a true relationship with Jesus Christ and thereby thwarting one of the greatest threats to the early church (Acts 9). Daniel used *prayer* to win over the powerful evil angels arrayed against him (Daniel 9). The early church *cried out in prayer* for ways of escape to be supplied for Peter when he was arrested and scheduled for execution (Acts 5, 12). Paul was delivered from the demonically induced rage of his attackers in Damascus by the *alertness* of the Christians that let him down in a basket outside the city (2 Corinthians 11:33). Commit these to memory and learn to apply them.

Truth

Righteousness

Peace

Faith

Salvation

Word of God

Prayer

Alertness

The Weapons of Righteousness Series

When we are facing the schemes of the Devil, he is trying to trip us up and rob us of the abundant life that Christ has planned for us. We need to know that Jesus Christ has provided spiritual weapons beyond just the Armor of God, which we extensively discussed in this book and also in my other book, *Secrets of the Armor of God*. He has given us all of the weapons of righteousness those for the right hand and for the left (2 Cor. 6:7). When we build these weapons into our life, we can thwart the work of the Devil and produce a life of good works and glory to God. Read and pray over the following list and see if there are any spiritual weapons that you need to develop. There are many, many resources that Principles to Live By offers to help you or your organization learn to use all that God has given you as a believer. *The Weapons of Righteousness* resources are listed below. All of which can be found at www.ptlb.com.

1. The Spiritual Disciplines
2. The Ten Foundational Doctrines of Christianity
3. Basic Spiritual Warfare: The Three Enemies and The Four Weapons
4. Closing Spiritual Doorways
5. The Armor of God
6. The Beatitudes: Christ-Like Behavior
7. God the Father: The Five Aspects of God
8. The Lord Jesus Christ: His Life, Death, and Resurrection
9. The Present Ministries of the Lord Jesus Christ
10. Knowing the Schemes of the Devil
11. The Holy Spirit: Empowering Believers Through Various Ministries
12. The Fruits of the Spirit
13. The Gifts of the Spirit
14. The Present Ministries of the Holy Spirit
15. The Bible
16. Salvation: Understanding and Using All Its Power
17. The Afterlife: Judgment Day, Heaven, and Hell
18. Biblical Meditation
19. Holy Angels
20. Testing: The Fruit, The Content, The Spirit
21. Great Commandments
22. The Boundaries of Love for You and Others (Ten Commandments)
23. A Loving, Righteous Husband
24. A Loving, Righteous Wife
25. A Loving, Righteous Marriage
26. A Maximized, Righteous Individual
27. A Loving, Righteous Family EPIC Parents - 5 "R" Kids
28. A Righteous Business
29. A Gracious, Ethical Employee

How to Use This Book

There are five ways that this material was designed for use. Originally it was to be used as an Intensive Discipleship curriculum for small groups of men or women to help them move significantly forward in their Christian lives. It can also be used for a personal devotion, mentor-directed study, a class format, or a sermon series with small groups. I have outlined how this could be conducted for each.

Small Group Study

1. Ask three to five people to join you to do this study. Participate in a small-group program within your church in which people are assigned to your small group to cover this material or develop your own group.

2. Set aside an hour to an hour and a half each week (or each month) to do the three crucial things required for spiritual life-change. First, discuss what happened when you practiced the spiritual exercises in the previous lesson. Second, learn about the next set of exercises and information. Third, take personal prayer requests from each member. This can often be most effective if it is done at breakfast or lunch in a restaurant before or during the workday or in the evening at a home. It doesn't have to be at church. In fact, many times it is better if it is not.

3. The time should be divided into three sections.

    a. The first 20-30 minutes should be spent sharing what happened when each person practiced the spiritual exercises that were assigned. Everyone must share even if they do not think that they were successful.

    b. The second 10-30 minutes are spent in learning the next week or month's lessons and exercises.

    c. The final 10-30 minutes are spent taking prayer requests from everyone. The prayer requests must be about the person themselves. This is not the time to have the group pray for a family member.

4. Each member of the group can read the book for further understanding of the information and exercises. The time spent together is not primarily a presentation time.

5. If one or more of the people have not tried or mastered the exercises, then the leader should feel free to repeat the same lesson again and again until this spiritual exercise is mastered.

6. If the group is meeting monthly, rather than weekly, then more exercises can be assigned. It can be helpful to have some form of accountability set up to make sure people are working on the exercises. This may be a daily or weekly e-mail stating what exercise they tried. The full explanation will come in the group time; but if everybody e-mails or texts what they are doing, then the group can stay on track.

Let's take a look at the first small group meeting:

1. Let everyone introduce themselves. A 60-second bio is usually helpful and lets everyone get to know everyone else.

2. Open in prayer.

3. Introduce the topic you will be exploring and pass out the books. Give an overview of the whole series.

4. Explain the first week or month's exercises.

5. Save 10-20 minutes for personal prayer requests.

The key to an effective discipleship group is not what the teacher says; it is what the disciple does. So give each person lots of time to tell about what happened when he or she started to practice the discipline. If the people in the group did not adequately try the discipline or did not see results from trying the discipline, then spend another week on that discipline. The goal of the group is not to get through the material within a specific amount of time but to develop new spiritual habits that will change their lives.

Personal Devotional Study

A second way to use this material is as a personal devotional study. In this format you can work through the material and look up the verses on your own, taking notes, practicing the exercises, and writing down your experiences for personal review. In this type of study you can proceed at your own pace. It may be one chapter a week, or it may be one chapter a day. The key is that the information is digested and the exercises are tried until some level of mastery is accomplished. It can be helpful to share your progress in this material with a mentor or spiritual accountability partner.

Let's take a look at what a personal devotional study would look like:

1. Open in prayer.

2. Read the material in the chapter.

3. Practice the exercise(s) suggested.

4. Record what you did and what happened when you did it. What will you continue to do because of using this exercise?

5. Practice the exercise again or in a different way until mastered.

Mentor-Directed Study

One of the most powerful ways of using this material is to ask a respected Christian you know to mentor you through this material. They do not need to do the study with you, but they do need to monitor and encourage you in the process of this study.

1. Ask a mentor to listen to your progress through this material once a month and pray for you as you explore these issues and exercises.

2. Meet the first time with your mentor and purchase a book for them so they can be tracking your progress. This meeting could be at a restaurant or a coffee house so that the meeting is more informal.

    a. Let them know what you are hoping to accomplish with this study and at what speed you would like to move through the material.

    b. Give them the freedom to teach, correct, rebuke, and train you as you move through the material

220

    c. Agree to meet monthly or weekly to hear updates on how you are doing. Remember, this is about you and not about them. They are mentoring you through this material and may not be going through it themselves. They are your spiritual guide, not a co-laborer.

    d. Have your mentor watch you pray or practice the exercise as they watch. They may be able to suggest ways to more effectively practice the spiritual exercise.

3. Ask your mentor to follow this format for your monthly or weekly sessions:

    a. Spend 20-30 minutes listening to what you have done and experienced as you have worked through the exercises.

    b. Listen to their insights and additions.

    c. Spend 10-20 minutes as they assign and explore the next chapter or re-assign the current material because they think there is a need to dwell on these ideas or habits more thoroughly.

    d. Spend 10-20 minutes giving the mentor three specific personal prayer requests you would like them to pray for until the next meeting.

4. Realize that your mentor may want to move off in tangents that are not directly tied to the material in this study guide, but that is what you want. They have life experience and spiritual wisdom that you want to be poured into your life. A mentor can often see mistakes or missteps that are about to take place when we cannot see them.

Class Format

A fourth way to use this material is in a class or mid-week teaching time at a church. The material that is contained in the book can be presented to a class, but it should take only about half the time allowed for the class. The other half of the time should be used for small groups to discuss what happened the week before when the discipline was tried. Also, allow for questions and prayer requests in regard to a growing spiritual life. This material should be repeated regularly as a part of a church's ongoing discipleship strategy. Every year, or every other year, a church can run one of these classes so that people are continuously moving forward.

The greatest danger to using this material in a class setting is that the teacher will use the whole time to present the material, not allowing adequate discussion of what happened when it was tried.

Second, there is the danger that it will be offered as new information only rather than as new practices or habits to incorporate into their life. The value of this material is in the exercises, not in the information. It is not possible to have a consistently deep walk with God without some of these disciplines being a part of their life. These materials are not just for delivering new information; they are to be practiced.

A third danger in using this material in a classroom setting is that the teacher or facilitator may not feel the freedom to repeat a discipline until all in the class have adequately tried it. There needs to be the freedom to go back over material that is not fully embraced until it has been adequately explored.

Let's take a look at what using this material in a classroom setting would look like:

Advertise the class in various places at church, work, or community. Let's take a look at what the first meeting of the classroom setting would look like:

1. Open in prayer.

2. Introduce an overview of the topic and pass out the books.

3. Let people know that this is an exercise/application-focused group, not a new information-focused group. They will learn new information but only so that they can then apply it to their life.

4. Introduce the first few exercises that will be tried in the first week or month.

5. Break the group into small groups for personal prayer requests.

For the remaining class periods, the following is the format for the standard meeting:

1. Open in prayer.

2. Give people 10-30 minutes to break into small groups of three or four and tell each other how the exercises from the last meeting went.

3. Spend 10-30 minutes explaining the new concepts and exercises to the group.

4. Put the group back into their small groups for personal prayer requests. Everybody has to share something that they want everyone to pray about.

Sermon Series and Small Groups

A fifth way to use this material is as a sermon series with accompanying small groups. This is where the whole church listens to the sermon series that the pastor is preaching, and then all small groups practice the material by doing the spiritual workouts at the end of each chapter. This is really a lab-lecture model of discipleship. It can be quite effective if the small group allows people to talk about trying the various disciplines. This is a way to jump-start Sunday morning attenders into people who are serious about developing spiritual habits. This multi-pronged approach can be very effective if there is adequate planning and opportunity for new groups to form even after the sermon series has started.

The goal of this book is for many Christians to begin practicing their Christianity and experiencing new levels of closeness with God. The process of walking with Christ takes time. The addition of new habits of life is essential. Expect that some will try these disciplines and then stop. Expect that others will have been waiting for this material for a long time and can quickly push to new depths with God. Patiently persevere. You and others will reap great joy in the presence of God.

About the Author

Gil Stieglitz is a catalyst for positive change both personally and organizationally. He excites, educates, and motivates audiences all over the world through passion, humor, leadership, and wisdom. He has led seminars in China, Europe, Canada, Mexico, and all over the United States.

In 1992, Dr. Gil founded the non-profit ministry *Principles to Live By* to help people and organizations win at life through biblical wisdom. Dr. Gil has been asked to repair, lead, and reinvigorate numerous organizations and individuals. He successfully led a church to 1,400% growth in a disadvantaged area. As a Denominational Superintendent in the Western United States, he led 50 churches and 250 pastors to over 300% growth. As a Superintendent of Schools, he oversaw a school system as it doubled in four years. As an executive pastor at a mega-church, he rebuilt a staff and added over one thousand people to its congregation. He injects dynamic life-change as a professor at universities and graduate schools on the West Coast and through seminars, sermons, and lecture series. He also partners with Courage Worldwide, a ministry that rescues young girls away from forced sexual slavery in America.

He has a B.A. from Biola University, as well as a Master's Degree and a Doctorate in Christian Leadership from Talbot School of Theology. He has authored over two-dozen books, manuals, and development courses including three best sellers. Dr. Gil's resources are available at Amazon.com as well as at www.ptlb.com.

Gil and his wife, Dana, have enjoyed over twenty-five years of marriage and reside in Roseville, California, where they raised their three precious girls.

Other Resources by Gil Stieglitz

Books:

Becoming Courageous

Breakfast with Solomon Volume 1

Breakfast with Solomon Volume 2

Breakfast with Solomon Volume 3

Breaking Satanic Bondage

Deep Happiness: The Eight Secrets

Delighting in God

Delighting in Jesus

Developing a Christian Worldview

God's Radical Plan for Husbands

God's Radical Plan for Wives

Going Deep In Prayer: 40 Days of In-Depth Prayer

Leading a Thriving Ministry

Marital Intelligence

Mission Possible: Winning the Battle Over Temptation

Proverbs: A Devotional Commentary Volume 1

Proverbs: A Devotional Commentary Volume 2

Satan and The Origin of Sin

Secrets of God's Armor

Spiritual Disciplines of a C.H.R.I.S.T.I.A.N

They Laughed When I Wrote Another Book About Prayer,
    Then They Read It

Touching the Face of God: 40 Days of Adoring God

Why There Has to Be a Hell

Podcasts

Becoming a Godly Parent

Biblical Meditation: The Keys of Transformation

Everyday Spiritual Warfare Series

God's Guide to Handling Money

Spiritual War Surrounding Money

The Four Keys to a Great Family

The Ten Commandments

**If you would be interested in having Gil Stieglitz speak to
your group, you can contact him through the website,
www.ptlb.com.**